Journey to Murder

Journey to Murder

Road to Forgiveness

by Jo Pollard

with D.J. Carswell

Authentic
LIFESTYLE

First published in 2001 by Paternoster Lifestyle
Reprinted 2002 by Authentic Lifestyle

08 07 06 05 04 03 02   8 7 6 5 4 3 2

Athentic Lifestyle is an imprint of Authentic Media,
PO Box 300, Carlisle, Cumbria, CA3 0QS, UK
and PO Box 1047, Waynesboro, GA 30830-2047, USA
www.paternoster-publishing.com

British Library Cataloguing in Publication Data

A catalogue record for this book is available from the British Library

ISBN 1-85078-409-4

Cover design by FourNineZero
Printed in Great Britain by
Cox & Wyman Ltd., Cardiff Road, Reading, Berkshire, RG1 8EX

To the memory of Michael.
Also to our three children:
Rebecca, Tamar and Andrew.

Acknowledgements

I want to say a special thank you
to the media for the positive encounters
I have had with them over the past three years.
Thanks also to
- Family, friends, neighbours and medical staff for their love and care
- Friends in Eastern Europe
- Christians around the world who have prayed for us
- Staff at Paternoster Publishing for their input and courage in helping me get into print
- Christine Watts, for transcribing my ramblings on tape
- Hazel Fenwick, for working so patiently throughout the project as personal assistant, typist and tea-maker and for being an encouragement at every stage.

Jo Pollard

To God be the glory.

Contents

Foreword

When I received the invitation to write a foreword for this book, I must confess my heart sank. It came when I was fleetingly in England between visits abroad and I was not looking for anything more to add to my daunting 'to do' list! But when I started flicking through the pages, I was completely 'hooked' and felt I wanted to explain why this book should be widely read.

There are three reasons why I commend this book.

First, it is a very 'good read'! The personal accounts of many adventurous journeys to the countries of Eastern and Central Europe are full of fascinating vignettes, written with such detail that readers will find themselves becoming travelling companions, sharing the journeys with this intrepid family, reliving their adventures, meeting their friends and sharing their anxieties, joys and, ultimately, their tragedy.

Secondly, readers who become their travelling companions will be inspired by the faith of this family - a faith which seems to prompt numerous 'miracles'. These are an encouragement to those who share the Christian faith; they demonstrate again and again how that faith in a God who can 'do exceedingly abundantly, above all we can ask or think' can be rewarded in ways beyond human imagination.

Thirdly, for potential readers who do not share the Christian faith, there is another message. The vivid descriptions of numerous journeys to free-spirited people behind the Iron Curtain, trapped in the vast prison created by Soviet Communism, are full of detail. Having undertaken many similar journeys myself taking aid to Poland and Romania in those dark days, this book brought back abundant memories of countless similar trials and tribulations. I will also never forget the courage, dignity, resilient humour and sacrificial generosity of the people whom we met there. More importantly, the book reminds all of us who have the privilege of living in freedom that we should not take our freedom for granted. The experiences of those subjected to totalitarian tyranny are not from a distant history or a remote corner of the earth. The people described in this book are very near to us, on the Continent of Europe, and they are our contemporaries. They remind us of our obligation to use our freedom in the service of those still imprisoned by tyrannical regimes in many parts of the world today.

Ultimately, this book is not just a book of travellers' tales. It takes the reader on a personal journey - a journey of faith in which the family who made it suffered many dangers and discomforts. The ending is not a happy one, in terms of this world's reckoning, but it is not a morbid or depressing story. For the human tragedy is just part of a larger picture: of a journey of life and death redeemed by love, where even human suffering and grief can be transformed by faith, hope and love - and by trust in the God who Himself suffered and died in order to bring the joy of resurrection to those who are prepared to walk in His way and to journey with Him to the end.

Caroline Cox
May 2001

Introduction

It was early morning. The driver of the bread van that was lumbering along the Hungarian road never imagined that his actions in the next few moments would later be reported by television and the media across Britain and other parts of the world.

The camper van at the roadside seemed unremarkable, but close to it a distressed woman was trying to flag down the passing vehicle. Her eyes were badly swollen. Her face was battered as though it had been kicked like a football. She staggered forward trying to push open her eyes, desperately trying to see out. As she approached she cried, 'I don't speak Hungarian, only English! I need the police! My husband is dead!'

Michael and Jo Pollard had been spending their annual summer holiday as they usually did, travelling through Eastern Europe. For almost thirty years they had risked their lives delivering basic necessities and Bibles to friends made over many years on such trips. On the night of August 4, 1997, while sleeping in their camper van in Hungary, they were attacked. Michael was left dead and Jo was badly injured. A passing van driver alerted the police. Jo was immediately taken to the Intensive Care Unit at a local hospital. From her hospital bed, the words she spoke in a telephone interview were broadcast on television and radio and heard by her family and friends and thousands of other listeners in Britain.

The fact that she was able to forgive in such terrible circumstances captured the imagination of press and public alike. Amidst personal suffering and grief, Jo had an inner peace. Her personal faith in 'the God who doesn't make mistakes' sustained her then and still motivates her in the aftermath of that fateful night. The story of her life takes her from one side of the world to the other. It includes rape, being held hostage and risking arrest in Eastern Europe, as well as carrying on her duties as an 'ordinary' housewife and teacher.

1

Birth of a Kiwi

Memories rise in the still air
Like smoke from many fires
(Rarawa Kerehoma)[1]

My first name really is Jo. Not Josephine or Josette - it's just Jo. My parents, Joseph and Vita Walker, named me Jo Valerie. They must have liked the names. I didn't like 'Valerie'; actually, I think it was my sister who wanted me to have it. I've never really got used to it and have always had difficulty with my name. So did the British press when they were reporting my husband's murder in 1997. They renamed me 'Solavalair'!

I was born at 8.00 a.m. on February 3 1942, the youngest of three children, in Whangarei, in the sub-tropical north of New Zealand. Polynesian voyagers named the land 'Tirititi ote Moana', the 'gift of the sea', and it was surely an idyllic place for any child to grow up in. The lavish scenery is filled with volcanoes, fjords, lakes, leaping geysers and lofty mountains, all competing to be the most spectacular. But just as the sun used to cast its long shadows across the green hills and paddocks, another more ominous shadow was to cast its cold darkness over my young life, that of being raped at the age of nine. I was only very young, but I knew that the man was doing something to my body that he should not. There are vague memories of being examined by a doctor, but I am not sure that I received any formal counselling. I think that I got over it fairly quickly at the time. It was only later, at the age of sixteen, that my mother disclosed more details of the attack. Apparently, after the man had raped me, his intention had been to strangle me and throw me in the river.

One of the fears I was left with was that of going out in the dark. Also, in later years, whenever a student invited me to go with him to the cinema in Auckland, then I would always find an excuse to bring along two or three other friends. I was frightened that something would happen to me again. It took me a long time to trust men.

In spite of this dreadful trauma the memories of my early years are, nonetheless, filled with the aroma and sweetness of innocence, just as fragrant as the roses on the three hundred bushes in our garden. I loved being able to run over the paddock to visit my grandmother, chasing the hens, and being with the animals. I was very much a tomboy and definitely happy as a child. I remember eating endless home-made ice cream seven days a week, looking for and catching tadpoles in our little pond and I can almost smell the creosote as I picture dad liberally using it to disinfect our primitive 'facilities'.

My parents were a study in contrasts. Dad was the quieter of the two, Mum the outgoing woman of many talents. A superb, innovative cook, she always served mouth-watering dishes to tempt our many visitors. I suppose it was from her that I learned to keep an 'open house'. From the beginning of our marriage, Michael and I wanted friends, neighbours - and strangers too - to feel welcome in our home, whether we were ready for them or not.

My mother, besides being a fantastic homemaker and 'mum' to her family, was also a fine pianist who accompanied many singers on our local radio station and the music festivals. Often she would go to town in the morning, buy material, pattern, buttons, thread, etc., to make an outfit for herself to wear in the evening. Busy as she was, she had perfected another art, beautiful copperplate handwriting. Often she was asked to copy some important document.

Mum gave Dad a big shock when he discovered that unknown to him, she had learned to drive and had even bought a car. Dad was a very reluctant passenger who never learned to drive, but eventually came round to travelling happily with her. There was a very good reason for Mum to have her own transport - public transport was inadequate and she wanted to take my handicapped brother, Kenny, to places he wanted to see.

Kenny was musical and brilliant at maths but he never fully recovered from the meningitis which struck him when he was two. As a young child I never knew how long he would live so I would worry about him if he was ever ill. Once he was knocked down on his way to school by a truck. Fortunately his injuries were not serious but I was very concerned because I loved my brother. He was a bit like my dad in that if he caught the flu or a similar infection, it was bad. I got on well with him - helping him to collect crickets in a jar! If he was being teased I would back him up, defending him in front of others.

My father was very proud of my mother and all her accomplishments. Though they were so very different, they seemed made for each other. He was fascinated by the stars, whose names he taught me, one by one, followed by the constellations and planets, which punched through those southern-hemisphere night skies. A 'man of the land,' he could also identify all sorts of flora and fauna. He combined a love of God's handiwork and artistry with a logical mind that could solve even the most difficult of maths problems (unfortunately his brilliance passed me by!).

We were never smacked as children. All my father had to do was to put his hand down to remove his slipper, which I suppose frightened me, but he never hit me or beat me or anything like that. Once, I remember, I painted the window ledges and father was not pleased! They were green but when he found out, the air was rather blue! Meanwhile I, had gone and put myself to bed thinking that he would come up and smack me, but he didn't.

I admired both my parents. Mum was not only 'quite a character' but also a very good mother. I would say I had a close relationship with my family but when I went back to England for the second time Dad just said goodbye to me as he always would in the morning. Then he simply set off. When I talked to my mum afterwards she said by way of explanation, 'I think he just knew that he would never see you again.' Dad and I got on very well and I was glad he was my dad! I wasn't hurt by his last farewell but I wanted to know why he acted as he did. Now I realize that it was probably breaking his heart that I was going again. He wouldn't have wanted anyone to see him in tears.

I didn't see him again. My parents didn't travel over to the wedding - dad was frightened of water as he didn't swim and did not like flying either. It would have been my mother only who would have attended. I think the reason she stayed at home was probably that she may have known deep down that dad was not very well. In 1969, not long after my marriage to Michael, she rang me to tell me he had died. I asked if I was to come home but she said not to because it was such a long distance to travel .

Mum was devastated by his death. She busied herself by moving to another part of Whangarei. Creative as ever, she designed and decorated her new house and even made a beautiful Japanese garden! But although she continued with her many different interests, she never really recovered from the loss of her husband. Her health deteriorated until the day when news reached me in England that she was gravely ill. I booked a flight to New Zealand, but she died while I was en route. I was able to attend her funeral, but I wish I had been there to say goodbye to her. She was a very remarkable woman.

My school years were, for the most part, happy ones, although I was unenthusiastic when my first day at primary school coincided with my birthday. As soon as my mother had waved goodbye to me, I climbed a fence intending to escape, but tore my new dress, which had been made especially for the occasion. As a last resort, mother bribed me with promises of ice cream; but she also made my big sister, Marjorie, keep watch on me just in case I made another frenzied escape. Now I come to think about it, I never did get that ice cream! But school improved as I learned, among other things, how to play the recorder and, later, the violin and flute.

When I was fourteen I was really excited to be able to go at last to the Easter youth camp with all my friends - altogether there were about fifty of us. The beautiful camp site was beside the Tasman Sea. On Easter Sunday we joined in a special service at a local church. I shall never forget singing of some of the old Easter hymns with choruses like 'Up from the grave he arose'. Despite attending church from as far back as I can remember it was really at that service that I understood for the first time the true significance of Jesus' death. In the evening the service was back at the camp site. The preacher was again explaining why Jesus had to die and rise from the dead. It was all very personal because up to that moment I would have said, 'Yes, Jesus did die for us' but that evening I realized that he had died for me. I knew then that it was not enough to just know about him - I had to ask the Lord to forgive me for the things that I had done wrong. A lovely lady named Ada spoke with me after the service about what I had heard. Together we prayed - it was then that the Lord Jesus Christ became my personal Saviour. At first I suppose I was a little embarrassed to tell people that I had become a Christian as I already went to church and was 'religious'; as time passed so did my embarrassment. I began to read my Bible more and also helped with Sunday School classes.

Eventually my turn came to 'fly the nest'. I didn't go too far at first. Ardmore Teacher Training College at Papakura, South Auckland had accepted my application to train for two years with them. Papakura is about 100 miles south of Whangarei and the campus was about twenty-five miles from the city. During the Second World War an air base was built there; at weekends many people came to fly small planes and gliders. Just down the road the army still had a camp. We even had a former grand prix racetrack. I once went round on a motorbike clinging desperately to my friend, who was driving. I was absolutely petrified. It was my first and last ride!

Those two years at college were brilliant. I joined the choir and orchestra. On Sundays, I regularly went to the evangelical Methodist Church. I really felt I was in the right place. Often in later teens, young people come face to face with the issues of life: 'Why are we here?' - 'Where are we going?' - 'What happens after death?' The higher education environment provides plenty of opportunities to explore new interests, make friendships and, for some, discover a relationship with God. I wanted to remain in Auckland to continue my music studies. Dorothy Hopkins and Cyril Howarth lovingly gave me singing and flute lessons. I suppose music has been one of those 'God-given gifts', which he has used in my life to share and tell the good news of Jesus to so many people.

I felt quite at home in my first post as a probationary teacher, although the school was in quite a rough area of the city. The reason was that the headmaster had also been head of my primary school in Whangarei; so although everyone else did one year and then moved on, I somehow managed to stay there three years, until in November 1963 I sailed over the horizon - en route to England!

2

Michael

'The gentle historian who dipped his pen in the milk of God's loving-kindness'[2]

Michael was a Yorkshireman who spoke with what some people might describe as a 'posh' accent. This tall, rather tousled teacher with his glasses, briefcase, old jacket, bundles of papers, and the ever-present diary, was my husband for twenty-eight years.

Michael Trevor Pollard was born on 28 May 1935 in Leeds. Ernest and Evelyn were very proud of their baby, who weighed in at 7 lbs. Meanwhile history, which was to be one of Michael's special interests, was playing out its drama amid the dark shadows of war and the bright lights of invention. 1935 was the year when: US rock and roll singer, Elvis Presley was born; the drums of war began to beat in Europe and in China the Long March of 200,000, led by Mao Tse Tung, ended, establishing him as undisputed leader of the hard-core Communists and a permanent threat to the Nationalist government.[3]

Michael was an only child, so his aunts and uncles featured prominently in his life. Arthur and Amy, now in their eighties, fondly remember him for his 'escapades'. He started school at New Farnley, near Leeds. Sitting at the desk in front of him was a young girl with long plaits. The temptation must have been too great for Michael who, having a pair of scissors in his hand, promptly cut off her plait. Hairdressing was definitely not allowed in the classroom.

Next-door neighbours Mr and Mrs Rawson had no children of their own, but experienced something of what this might have been like had Michael been theirs. Later, Michael would learn that 'to everything there is a season - a time to plant and a time to pluck up what is planted', but one day, while Mr Rawson worked hard furrowing and planting his crop of potatoes, Michael, knowing nothing of the time lapse between sowing and planting, followed behind him, diligently unearthing the entire crop!

The aroma of freshly baked bread often filled the family home. Michael's mother would leave the dough to rise near the fire while she busied herself elsewhere. Three days in succession Michael had to explain how the dough had mysteriously jumped out of the bowl and embedded itself well and truly in the carpet.

But a later school report from West Leeds High School indicates a desire to study. Headmaster J. S. Barnshaw commented on his politeness, noting that 'he contributed much to school life in games and debates . . . his hobbies are wide and sensible . . . he has a good brain'. He mentioned other qualities, significant in Michael's early and later life: '[His] placid exterior conceals an enthusiasm and capacity for work which tends to sweep away all obstacles to progress. He has a whimsical sense of humour and plenty of imagination.'

After graduating at Sheffield University, he went to Hull to train as a teacher. He supplemented his grant with his earnings as a market researcher for the BBC; this helped pay for his hobbies, which included brass rubbing and rugby league.

Michael taught in schools in both the public and private sector. Although he spent his whole working life in Yorkshire he was a keen youth hosteller and often took school parties of children on trips not only in Great Britain, but also to Greece, Poland, Denmark, Andorra and France. However, he was not a 'practical' man. Before we married he assured me that he could cook. But one of his pupils, Ann Owen, (née Sharpe), remembers sharing his lunch when he was teaching at St Phillip's in Burley-in-Wharfedale: 'The school party was plodding across a moor in winter. We were very tired, hungry, wet and cold. We took shelter in a cow shed and were given some of Michael's famous sandwiches - two slices of bread with lumps of butter, and in the middle - meat paste! I took my own sandwiches after that.' No wonder the sandwiches were 'famous'. I suspect the reason he invited me to go youth hostelling with him may have been so that I could do the cooking.

Another St Phillip's pupil, Eric Clarkson, also remembers a school party, although for rather different reasons. When he was twelve, Michael encouraged him to join the Historical Society: 'This was the start of some remarkable and personality-developing experiences. Perhaps I should have been more selective after my first outing, which was to see the Roman ruins at Aldborough near Boroughbridge. Six of us set off with Michael in his Ford Anglia. In Otley, Michael leapt out of the car without a word and ran up to an unsuspecting member of the public. Thrusting a clipboard under his nose, Michael proceeded to question him about his TV viewing habits (I found out later that he was doing this to supplement his meagre salary). This done, Michael joined us in the car and we sped off on our journey. Michael had a way of heightening the excitement of a trip by educating us with some background knowledge of the area. By the time we reached Harrogate the atmosphere in the car was electric with stories of past visits to exotic destinations, taking in trips to "treacle mines" etc.! We pulled up at the library to find another six children waiting to go with us as well. We all piled into Michael's Ford Anglia - six in the back, five in the front, including Michael, and one in the boot - held open by a tin of baked beans! With present-day laws plus the huge volume of traffic on the roads no teacher would do this nowadays, but that was a different age. The atmosphere in the car by now was supercharged - a melting pot of jokes, quips, laughter, leg-pulling and serious thoughts about the purpose of our journey. The trips also included a detour by the post office to try and find Gwen Topham (a distant relative of the Tophams who owned Aintree racecourse). This was my introduction to Michael, the man! What he offered children in those days may have been considered irresponsible by some, but I am eternally grateful.'

A number of his pupils kept in touch. Although Michael the teacher was not a 'disciplinarian', he inspired affection. According to Ann Owen, he 'could not control the class much, so we "took the mickey" and teased him unmercifully, but he took it in good faith'. But she remembers him as 'a very interesting teacher'.

Richard Longstaff, a neighbour and friend, who was also taught R.E. and Maths by Michael at Ladderbanks Middle School in Baildon, remembers him as 'a wise "old" man, who was always wholeheartedly approachable in my hour of informative need. Depending on the flippancy of our mood in the classroom, I would occasionally dare to call him by his famous nickname, "Percy". In hindsight, I feel this is a lasting reflection of the goodness of his character, the fact that he would never erupt, and in principle would never say boo to a goose.'

Stuart Shepherd, now in charge of crisis management with Wycliffe Bible Translators, and a lifelong friend of ours, recalls how he first met Michael - a meeting which transformed Michael's life. 'I was on holiday in North Wales at Llandudno; actually I was an unpaid volunteer with United Beach Missions, a Christian group from different churches, mostly young people, who during the summer share their faith and trust in Jesus Christ with children and families at various resorts around the country. One of the men on the team was giving a public talk about the good news of Jesus, and Michael had stopped and was listening intently. Mike was eager to talk when I introduced myself to him. I remember thinking how sad it was that this young man was on holiday without a friend (ironically though, hundreds were to pay their respects to him at his funeral). Mike was happy to stay and chat about the gospel message he had just heard. We sat down right there on the sea front and read a few verses from the Bible - we even prayed together . . . We saw a lot of Mike that week. He showed up for tea and some of the activities. My wife Mary and I were also from Leeds so when we all returned from the holiday we kept in touch. Michael became a Christian. My contact with Mike after that was every four or five years as I had moved to the USA with my work. When I returned to Leeds, I can remember thinking, "This is the man who seemed so sad and lonely on holiday - he is now utterly transformed." He was a new creature altogether because of Christ's work in his life. Mike never stopped to think if he was gifted, he simply saw a need - saw needy people who were without Christ and was available with what gifts God had given him.'

Michael kept a diary, which he would produce at various times to record - who knows what? Michael's handwriting was atrocious and totally illegible to all but its author. Sadly, we have no record of his final thoughts, though we do have a few specimens of his tiny diaries. Many have tried to decipher his writing but to no avail. His private thoughts have been securely deposited in the bank of eternity and only God has the keys.

3

New life - new wife!

For better, for worse, for richer for poorer,
In sickness and in health, to love, cherish and to obey,
Till death us do part. (Book of Common Prayer)

As a child I had been an avid reader of Enid Blyton. I dreamed about going to England to see all the things she had written about. There were about eighteen of us at school who decided we would all go on the same ship to England. In the end I was the only one who went. Not by air, of course - in the mid-twentieth century air travel was neither so common nor so cheap as today. The only other option was the ocean liner and after six weeks at sea I was glad when the ship finally docked. At Victoria Station I was met by a penfriend with whom I had been corresponding ever since I was eleven years old. He took me to stay with his mother in London. I had no job but was not particularly worried about this.

Back home in New Zealand, my mother was in town one day when she met the mother of one of my school friends, Sheila, who, as it turned out, was also in England. Sheila was on what was described as 'a working honeymoon', living in Normanton and working in Ferrybridge, West Yorkshire. Mum passed the news on to me so I made contact with Sheila. In consequence, I moved up to Yorkshire, having applied to do some supply teaching to replace a teacher whose husband was dying of cancer. I wasn't at the school for long but I made many friends and kept in touch with the headmaster and his wife for a long time.

Although I did move back to London for a while, I eventually gravitated to Yorkshire - famous for so much, including cricket, beautiful countryside, fish and chips at Harry Ramsdens, also (remember, this was 1964!) coal mining and flat caps. 'Miners' meant 'music' in Yorkshire as well as Wales, and my enthusiasm led me to join a choral society, and to sing in the choir of the church I joined. One day a dapper little man called at my lodgings in Ilkley. He was both a vicar and the headmaster of a small independent school at Burley-in-Wharfedale. He knew about me because the wife of the man who conducted the choral society taught there, and he offered me a teaching job until Christmas. It wouldn't be for long, I thought, but having a job would mean money in my pocket. As things turned out, he extended the offer and I taught there until the end of the school year, when I returned to New Zealand.

This was how I found myself at the same school as Michael. It took pupils of up to sixteen years of age and he was teaching Religious Education. At first he didn't really have much to do with me and kept his distance. Our first contact was anything but romantic - gradually we found ourselves eating school lunches together before he dashed off to play cricket. I learned that he often took students on trips, staying at youth hostels. He invited me along too, although, as I have said, I suspect this was mainly so that I could do the cooking. Our friendship developed in a natural and non-threatening way. We were working together in a small school and we shared a number of interests, such as travelling and the theatre. In time we went to the theatre together and made a visit to his parents, but it was always just as friends. The fact that Michael did not 'rush things' at all helped me to learn to trust him. Michael was gentle and stable, not a dynamic man, but very kind. Some people might have described him as 'ordinary', but that was just the type of person I needed. My rape attack as a young girl had left scars and I was fearful of men in general. I needed someone I could trust completely; Michael was to be that man.

I had planned to return to New Zealand in 1965 but things didn't prove as straightforward as I had hoped. The fare was a bit of a surprise; two years earlier my ticket to England had cost £6 - the return would be £14! But this wasn't a serious problem. The real difficulty arose because a Greek shipping company had lost one of its ships, the *Laconia*, with all hands, in the Atlantic. The company replaced it with another vessel, the Dutch liner, *Willem Ruys* - the very ship on which I had booked my return passage. So instead of taking a sea voyage I went overland by bus with a friend from Ilkley.

It was an amazing experience for both of us. Turkey, Syria, Jordan, Lebanon, Iran and Iraq provided us with cultural experiences we would never forget. Afghanistan and a trip to the Khyber Pass were on the itinerary, but regrettably India and Pakistan were not getting on too well so we were re-routed. A third-class train journey without lights, a plane to Bombay and a ship via Penang, Singapore and various Australian ports finally brought us, a little exhausted, to the last leg of the journey, which was by plane. I so looked forward to being back home and especially visiting some of my former Bible class friends. In fact they were there to meet me at the airport. As I stepped out, there on the tarmac I saw the wonderful red carpet that had been laid out . . . for me? It turned out to be intended for royalty. Queen

Salote of Tonga had died in New Zealand. Actually, I remembered her. She used to come to New Zealand for three months every year and while staying at Government House worshipped at our church. The minister would welcome her the first Sunday, but the rest of the time she was treated as an ordinary member of the congregation. She was a lovely person.

While I was in New Zealand, there was an important development in my relationship with Michael. He started writing to me - every week. When I came back to the house where I was staying, I would find a message from my housemates - 'Cupid has written!' - and then have to control my impatience as I searched to discover where the letter had been hidden.

One letter brought news of a remarkable development. Shortly after I left, Michael's father had died. He and his mother took a short holiday break in Llandudno. There, he told me, he had met someone from United Beach Missions (Stuart Shepherd, who later became one of our close friends). He had asked Michael if he was a Christian and Michael had replied, 'I've read the Bible through twice, pray every day and go to church.' Stuart encouraged him to join a Bible study group when he returned home to Leeds. As his church didn't have one he went along to one at the home of a local G.P., Dr Eileen Frankland, who later gave him a birthday present which accompanied us on our travels.

During these times together with others in Calverley, Michael heard about the visit to England of the American evangelist, Dr Billy Graham. Michael went to help at one of his meetings, which was being relayed to a hall in Otley. That night he realized that although he was religious he had never been 'born again'. So he put things right between him and God. His letters to me showed a change, something was different about him.

He had a real experience of God, which permeated all his life.

During our correspondence Michael had indicated he was looking forward to my return and when I got to Yorkshire he was still there. But although we went to a number of Christian meetings together he seemed rather dilatory about our relationship. In the end I decided that if he didn't propose I would go to Scotland, Ireland or Cornwall, to discover my family roots. I explained that I would have to get in touch with the Home Office because my permitted time in the United Kingdom was running out. That clinched it. Michael proposed, we got engaged on Christmas Day (the sole content of my Christmas stocking that year was an engagement ring) and the rest, as they say, is history!

Plans were made for a summer wedding. My dress was made by my very clever mother in New Zealand and I anxiously watched for the postman every day to see if he was bringing that all-important parcel. What if it got lost? The big day drew nearer. Still nothing had arrived. I confess I was worried. Michael's headmaster came to my rescue by assuring me, 'Look, if it doesn't arrive in time, you can use my daughter's wedding dress.' Fortunately, the Royal Mail didn't let me down and I was spared the ignominy of having to wear another's bridal robe. On my way to the hairdresser on the day of the wedding, my sense of humour got the better of me. I stopped off at a post office, wrote a telegram to Michael and sent it to the reception: 'CONGRATULATIONS ON EXCELLENT CHOICE OF WIFE - JO.'

As my father could not attend the wedding, I asked a friend to stand in for him. Mr Lythe was the manager of a local shoe shop, Freeman Hardy and Willis. His wife taught at the same school as me in Ilkley as well as attending Wells Road Methodist church. They had kindly invited me to stay at their home on many occasions.

It was June 7 1969 when Michael and I exchanged our wedding vows at South Parade Baptist Church, Headingley, Leeds - 'until death us do part'.

4

The unwelcome visitors

'When you hear the national anthem you will know it is all over.'
So said a Radio Prague announcer delivering the epitaph of free Czechoslovakia.
Over his words came the sound of gunfire.
His voice breaking with emotion, he told the world, 'Let our last words be engraved on your memory.'[4]

Teaching has very few perks but the best of these are the holidays! Michael and I were part of the intrepid breed of 'youth hostellers'. The camaraderie found among fellow travellers was a welcome diversion from the rigours of classroom teaching. In 1968, the year before our marriage, our itinerary was to include a trek across Europe to Czechoslovakia, visiting Prague, Brno and Bratislava.

It was our third evening in the wonderful city of Prague. With our group, we had enjoyed a very pleasant cultural evening at the famous Black Theatre. The others wandered off to a beer garden but it was already late, so Michael and I strolled back to the hotel where we were staying, there being no hostels in Prague in 1968. Exhausted, I promptly fell fast asleep in the downstairs room I was sharing with two other women. Michael however had no key and couldn't get into his room until the revellers returned. He was so tired he fell asleep as he was, on the stairs. Later, someone woke him and gave him a key. He crawled into bed and eventually fell asleep again - but not for long.

As his room-mates returned Michael couldn't help overhearing what they were saying.

'I wonder what we have done to offend them!'

'How far is it to the border?'

'How fast do tanks travel?'

This was enough to waken Michael! He said nothing but as the others drifted off to sleep, Michael pondered the wider implications of their words. He realized that what he heard implied the end of the so-called 'Prague Spring'.

The 'Prague Spring'

When Alexander Dubcek took over as Czech Communist leader at the beginning of 1968 the whole country, and especially Prague, was launched into an exhilarating 'springtime' of freedom. This new-found freedom was displayed in various ways. There was more real news available on TV, radio and in the papers. There was open criticism of low wages, bureaucratic oppression and poor housing conditions. Corruption in high places was exposed. Dubcek however continued to insist that Czechoslovakia would remain an ally of Russia. Dubcek's programme was, as people said, to give socialism a 'human face'. But meanwhile Soviet forces were massing just across the border.

On 20 August 600,000 Soviet, East German, Polish, Hungarian, and Bulgarian troops invaded and occupied the country. Although about 25 Czechs and Slovaks were killed, resistance was generally non-violent. Dubcek, who had always believed the Soviets would not invade, was appalled. 'How could they [the Soviets] do this to me?' he cried. 'My entire life has been devoted to co-operation with the Soviet Union. This is my own profound personal tragedy.' He was among the reform leaders who were abducted to the USSR. The Prague Spring of freedom was becoming the Moscow winter of oppression.

As dawn broke over Prague's magnificent buildings and monuments on August 22, Michael heard the drone of military planes. Looking out from his bedroom window he saw soldiers with parachutes, floating down like khaki confetti, making their abnormal entry to the capital city. Meanwhile, I was sleeping 'the sleep of the just', blissfully unaware of the tragedy that was unfolding throughout that beautiful country. Although that day was certainly no holiday for the citizens of Prague, nevertheless it was still *our* vacation, invasion or no invasion. Michael and I decided to explore the capital regardless of all the tanks, army vehicles, anti-aircraft weapons and thousands of foreign troops. There was a petition, which we dutifully signed, demanding the release of the Czech president and others involved in the Prague Spring, and that the invaders return home.

Three days later we were given our marching orders. Travelling by train to Germany, we reflected on our adventure. At Frankfurt, the Salvation Army met us and kindly watched over us as we slept, with our heads resting on a table. To be honest, Michael and I would have preferred to complete our holiday, especially as we had seen history being made. It had been quite exciting, even if it had been a little dangerous! Little did we realize the 'excitement' and 'danger' of the adventures God had planned for our lives in the years that followed!

5

The encourager and the Bible smuggler

'Who is my neighbour?' (Luke 10:29)

Family life

Our first and only home was in Baildon, West Yorkshire. This is where we spent our married life and brought up our children, Rebecca, Tamar and Andrew. When I was expecting my first child, I gave up teaching, never to return to it until Andrew, the youngest, was at nursery school. At that time a former colleague needed someone to cover for maternity leave so I gladly resumed my career. I liked babies! I enjoyed looking after them, although I always hankered after twin girls for some reason! Despite being an only child, Michael was quite good with the children although he left much of the day-to-day care of the children to me, but I didn't mind.

Sadness

Mark was our second child; I remember the day he first moved inside my womb. Towards the end of the pregnancy, the doctors felt sure my dates were wrong. They kept telling me that this was going to be 'a big baby'. At that time, there was much controversy over the number of women 'induced' into labour. Many women alleged that hospitals were increasingly doing this for the convenience of the staff rather than for specific medical conditions. (I remember contributing my thoughts about this on a BBC Radio Four programme.) Eventually I too was induced; the doctors decided to bring forward the delivery by five weeks due to 'the size of my baby'. Mark was born on 26 November 1974. He was 6lb 10oz - hardly a 'big baby' - and although he survived birth he lived for only three days.

That period was a double tragedy for me, because in January 1975 a telegram arrived informing me that my brother Kenny had died in the home where he had been placed. The incident was reported as an 'accident' but there had been a lot more to it than that and the staff member responsible was subsequently dismissed. So things were quite tough for a while in our personal lives; nevertheless we had to carry on with our jobs as best we could.

Activities

At school, life was as busy as ever. Michael still pursued his interests in history and rugby as well as attending Christian conferences from time to time. As Christians, we started to regularly attend a local church. Together we began what was to become our lifelong practice of making many friends all over the country and also abroad. At the famous Keswick Bible Convention, held annually in the town of that name, surrounded by the beauty of the Lake District, we met some friends who were to be the means of our meeting a man who was to change our lives.

It was 1969 and Michael and I were visiting these friends. After welcoming us they kept asking us to keep our voices down, as 'Andrew' was asleep. We thought nothing much of their request, thinking that probably their young son was tired; so we were surprised to learn that 'Andrew' was no less a person than 'Brother Andrew', the mysterious figure known as 'God's Smuggler'. Few would have guessed that the life of this tall lean young man with a Dutch accent was in constant danger. His 'Open Doors' mission involved him in travelling discreetly throughout what were then known as the 'closed' Communist countries of the world, criss-crossing their borders in order to deliver Bibles to Christians, many of whom were suffering for their faith. (During the sixties and on until Communism collapsed in Europe, it was often illegal for Christians to meet for worship, to own a Bible, or encourage others to become Christians. Publishing or distributing the Scriptures was forbidden and yet the Bible, God's written Word to us, is a real necessity for Christians. There are many horrific but well-documented stories of how individuals suffered for their faith during that time. Today such persecution continues elsewhere in the world, particularly in China and some Islamic countries and it is not unknown in parts of the Russian Commonwealth of Independent States.)

We told Brother Andrew about our exciting experiences in Czechoslovakia, the previous summer, when for a few days we had glimpsed a little of the oppression suffered by people living under extreme political regimes. He reminded us of 1 John 3:16,17: 'We know love by this, that he [Jesus] laid down his life for us - and we ought to lay down our lives for one another.' How does God's love abide in anyone who has the world's goods and sees a brother or sister in need and yet refuses help?. He challenged us, as teachers with long holidays, to use our time in making innocent trips to 'closed' countries taking with us gifts of Bibles, food and medicines for needy, suffering Christians.

This was a means by which people, who had never dreamed of being missionaries, could play a role greater than anything that had previously been done. Smuggling in a large carload of Bibles was risky, but most border guards would say nothing to a single copy in the local language, among a traveller's personal effects. In this way a thousand tourists could be a thousand ambassadors of God. These tourists would not only visit the museums and the factories, but would seek out the places, often small and out of the way, where Christians met to worship.

6

If God wants you there, He'll lead you to the people

Guide our feet into the way of peace. (Luke 1:79)

Brother Andrew's words had made us think. And so the big decision was made. We would spend our summer holidays exploring Eastern Europe. But where and how? And whom would we meet? We had no contacts. Someone encouraged us: 'If God wants you there, he will guide you to the people.' That is exactly what he did.

Our first trip as 'unofficial aid distributors' was to Czechoslovakia and Hungary. Soon we had explored Yugoslavia, Romania, Bulgaria and even Russia. Technically, we were never really smugglers. It's true that we did take in things that were classed as prohibited imports in the countries which we visited, but they were only medicines, food, and Christian literature. Nor did our vehicle have any 'secret compartments' as such. On the other hand, camper vans are built to make maximum use of space and every cupboard or hole, every nook and cranny, was filled with our gifts, all of which could be inspected at any time by border guards or secret police.

Looking for Evan Cirkev

In the early days of travelling in Czechoslovakia, we were given two or three addresses by a student from Bradford University who was studying Russian in Presov, near the Russian border. We hadn't been there before, so we were very pleased to have the new contacts, among them 'Evan Cirkev'. As we made our way across to Slovakia, we enjoyed the beauty of the Tatra mountains and the lovely countryside. We arrived in Presov and easily found the address of 'Evan Cirkev'. But the man who answered the bell looked very perplexed, even when we showed him the name and address we had been given. So we took our leave and walked round and round the town trying to find another street of the same name, but without success. Then in the evening, as we were thinking about finding somewhere to sleep, we saw people with Bibles so we decided to follow them. They had come for a Bible study but we didn't speak Slovakian, so we didn't understand very much. But a mystery was solved. We were overjoyed to learn that we had actually found 'Evan Cirkev'. No wonder the man at what turned out to have been the correct address didn't know what we wanted. 'Evan Cirkev' wasn't a man at all but simply short for 'Evangelical Church'!

Once we spent a couple of nights on the Yugoslav border with a family who told us of a large service in Romania at which about one hundred people were baptized as believers. This was in the early seventies and there was no way of getting addresses of Christians. The Securitate, the Romanian secret police, were watching everyone. But we were encouraged by this information, and felt sure we would have no problems in finding Christians galore once we set foot in Romania. So we crossed the border, heading for Timosoara. But despite spending most of the day endlessly walking up and down the streets, we could not find one Protestant church. Finally, we gave up on Timosoara. The next place we would try was the capital, Bucharest. By then, darkness had closed in. Michael and I decided we should make camp in Timosoara for the night so we found a field by the river and slept outdoors, beneath the stars. That may sound very romantic, but unfortunately we were not alone. The mosquitoes saw us coming - to them we were supper and breakfast!

The little blue book

Michael made a habit of setting aside a few moments each day to read, reflect and pray. Whether it was before a hectic school schedule or before embarking on one of his overseas jouneys or just on ordinary days at home, out would come the little blue copy of 'Daily Light'. This dog-eared book, measuring three by five inches, was Michael's constant companion for practically thirty years. First issued in 1794, *Daily Light for the Daily Path* (to give it its full name) contains selections of verses - sometimes just sentences - taken from various parts of the Bible, for each morning and evening. While newer updated copies adorned the shelves of many bookshops, Michael preferred the well-loved and well-thumbed edition he had been given as a birthday present by Dr Eileen Frankland in 1968. Covered at some stage in its much-travelled life in sixties-style blue-green plastic, it has survived its trans-European journeys with the aid of Sellotape. Today its edges are stained brown and its bent spine bears the sign of old age. Although the battered little book was near to retirement, it was still in full employment despite its outward decay. That night in the field in Romania was no exception. As usual, Michael took it out and read some words from St Mark's Gospel: 'Come aside by yourselves to a deserted place and rest awhile' (Mark 6:3). There were also words from 2 Corinthians 6:17: 'Come out from among them and be separate.' We certainly were outside - with the mosquitoes! We were also separate as we knew no one in the country!

Next morning, we were anxious to get to Bucharest as soon as we could, to try to find a Baptist church. Up and down the streets we drove until at last we found one - which turned out to be Lutheran. 'Well, it doesn't matter', we thought, ' they're bound to tell us where to find the Baptist church.' Our spirits lifted again as we saw the minister. 'Please could you give us directions to the Baptist church?' we asked him.

'No, I'm very sorry, I can't.'

'But could you tell us where the other churches are, please?'

'Try the telephone book.'

It was obvious that the poor man was extremely frightened. So we thanked him and set off to try to find a hotel. The hotel was much easier to find and, as we hoped, it had a telephone directory. Within no time, we had found a list of the churches, obtained a map of the area, and arrived at the church at about midday. People kindly made room for us, men on one side and women on the other. At a rough estimate, there were about two thousand people in the congregation. The service had started at 9 a.m. and was due to finish at 1 p.m. At the end of the service, Michael leaned over and whispered to me, 'The man sitting next to me has just wrapped something in a newspaper. I wonder if it's a Bible?' The man turned to us and, in perfect English, to our chagrin said, 'Yes, actually it is!'

Apparently, churches were only allowed to hold services only on Saturday night and Sunday morning, except for one little church, which had special permission. On Sunday mornings German-speaking Christians used the building, followed in the afternoon by the Romanian speakers. The man who spoke English was our first contact. He took us to the afternoon service but before he left us, Michael asked him if he would like some books in Romanian. As the man took the books, his face just lit up with excitement. 'Do you know? It was I who translated these books into Romanian! Although I did the work, I have never seen a copy until today!'

Much later, we were to discover that Constantin was one of the most prominent Christians in Romania. Several times he was imprisoned for being a Christian. Despite being tortured and behind bars for many years, he kept his faith. Wherever he was, he shared the good news about Jesus Christ. Between us, we devised a special code for his letters so that he could secretly let us know if he was in prison. He is still alive and we keep in touch. Nowadays, with the new religious freedoms, he regularly visits people in the very prison where he was incarcerated.

7

On the road

Remember the poor. (Galatians 2:10)

We became convinced that God did want us to work in Romania; over the next few visits he led us to so many key Christians. They were able to guide us, teaching us how to be effective and useful amongst the thousands of desperately poor and needy people. Some, who were very strong and brave, went to their governments to ask for less pressure to be put on Christians - even for permission to publicly own their faith. Many were beaten. Some were imprisoned. The situation deteriorated but they continued to trust in their Saviour, being faithful to him. One such person, Pavel, asked if he could travel with us to a place called Resita, near Timosoara. We were very happy to have him with us, as he would be able to speak in Romanian if necessary. He was a real 'character'. Often he would wave out of the window or stop to chat to people as we went by, speaking to any whom he recognized as being Christians.

On most trips, we seemed to have some sort of vehicle breakdown! Michael was not very mechanically-minded but usually managed to cope. So as usual, problems with the vehicle meant that we had a slow journey to Resita. It was very, very late when we arrived. In addition we were absolutely exhausted. We searched for the address where Pavel was expecting to stay, but without success. In the end, he decided to knock on the door of a flat where there was a light. He would take the risk of asking a stranger if he could stay the night, in the hope of finding his friends the next day.

We were all right because we could sleep in the Dormobile. After parking on the pavement, we made up our bed and were asleep in no time. In the morning we were woken up by a knock on the door. Our first thoughts were that it was the secret police being not so secret but thankfully we were mistaken. A young man spoke to us in Romanian, then, realizing that we could not understand him, tried again in French. He was inviting us to breakfast! When we followed him upstairs to the family flat the first thing we saw was an open Bible on the table. Then we heard the sound of Christian music from the record that was playing (no CDs for many years yet!). To our utter amazement we understood that we had actually parked outside the very place we were looking for.

Today, years after the end of the cold war, Communism has collapsed and border restrictions have been relaxed; it is hard to imagine just what it was like to travel through Eastern Europe in the seventies and eighties. As you left West Germany with its fast cars, bright lights and shops full of consumer goods, you suddenly found you were being made to crawl along a 'corridor' of concrete until you reached the checkpoint crossing. All around were watchtowers with armed guards who never smiled. Menacing barbed wire spiked any place that could have afforded an escape. As their vehicles were examined, travellers felt the chill of fear. Questions were thrust in faces and endless patience was needed to queue for hours and hours for petrol coupons or to change money. Even after passing the searching scrutiny of the soldiers, drivers faced long journeys over poor roads, where sudden speed restrictions were strictly enforced by armed men. You would often see police or soldiers standing in the middle of the road monitoring your approach through their binoculars. You dared not make a mistake, knowing that the fines would be instant and outrageous.

Michael was very astute in all his dealings with what might be described as the 'less than democratic' countries through which we travelled. Every day he made tiny jottings in his diary (but never entered any detail that could betray contacts). He would memorize the complicated names and addresses of an ever-growing list of families who relied on our supplies. Those that he couldn't recall he wrote down in invisible ink. What a treasure of insights and memories lie hidden there in writing so tiny and indistinct that no one can decipher them.

A handful of memories

Plunging my hand into the 'bran tub' of our experiences, I have picked out a handful of memories, which depict some aspects of life in the Eastern bloc in those Communist days.

The matchbox toy

The house was extremely poor, by anyone's standards. There was only one light bulb and if someone moved from one room to another at night they had to take the light bulb with them. The toilet was down the back of the garden and of course there was no light there. The family grew their own corn and although they had hens and ducks which they used for food, the soup-like meals were flavourless and more like water. Although we always took our own food supply so that we wouldn't have to deplete their already meagre supplies, Romanian Christians are extremely hospitable and invariably insisted on feeding us too. We felt guilty about this because they would want to give us anything they had, even their last slice of bread. They had so little yet they were so kind and generous. It was a practical lesson to us all.

It was our first visit to Constanta in Romania. We had been invited to stay with a family we had not met before, though we were acquainted with other members of the family. As we were getting our nightclothes and other things from the boot of our Skoda car, we felt that someone was watching us. It was the couple's young son. His sharp eyes followed our every movement with great interest. Then something caught his attention and he stood transfixed. When we looked in the boot to see what had caught his eye we soon discovered what it was.

To understand the incident fully, I must go back to when Michael was teaching at Beckfoot Grammar School in Bingley. It had been one of those 'trying' days that teachers get from time to time and one boy in particular had been messing about with something, distracting the class when really he should have been concentrating on the joys of history. After warning him, Michael had to confiscate the offending item - a matchbox toy. The boy was told to collect it at the end of the week. But either he forgot as did Michael, or he was too embarrassed to ask for it since he was fifteen years old and to be found playing with a little toy car would damage his 'street-cred'. It had been Michael's last term at

Beckfoot and he was to start at a new school in September. It was highly unlikely that he would be able to trace the boy again.

Time had buried the little car amongst the Pollard junk in our car boot, only to be found months later, by a young Romanian boy. Michael decided to give our young friend the matchbox car. It turned out that he had never had a toy in his life! As a result, we often took toys to children who were deprived and without toys of their own.

The rainbow man

The brightly lit petrol stations we know in the West, with mini-shops selling anything from sweets to soap powder, milk to magazines, and car accessories to fast food, are a far cry from the petrol stations of Eastern Europe in the days of Communism.

For one thing there were so few of them. They were carefully noted on maps so we could estimate how long our thirsty camper van would need to survive. Often if we wanted to buy petrol we had to have special coupons, which inevitably had to be queued for at the border. (Queuing was a national sport of most countries!) Sometimes the petrol supply was restricted, sometimes there was none at all. Breakdowns were a constant hazard! We got used to seeing Trabants and little Fiats, with bonnets up, resting at the roadside and looking like injured birds nursing broken wings.

We were on our way back to Bohemia via friends in Slovakia. I had noticed the map showed a petrol station that wasn't too far ahead, so suggested that we fill up. At first Michael said that we should be all right but then changed his mind, deciding that he might as well get some, 'just in case'. He pulled in behind another vehicle, then came back to me and said, 'I think the man in front of us is a Christian, he has a rainbow with a cross on the back window of his car.' We got chatting with the driver, who spoke very good English and turned out to be from a Pentecostal church, which in those days was a forbidden denomination. We exchanged names and addresses. From then on we visited him whenever we were in Slovakia. In fact, his was to be the last house we visited before Michael's murder.

Albania: The country that forgot God

Michael and his Spanish friend Arnaldo were very in-terested in Albania, which the (then) political leader, Enver Hoxha, claimed was the first atheistic state. They decided to make a trip there one Easter. It was extremely risky for Christians. So we knew that such a trip had to be undertaken with the utmost care. I was under the impression that Michael and his friend weren't taking any Christian literature with them, but they did - I suspect they didn't want to worry me!

The searches both entering and leaving Albania were very thorough and intimidating. Michael and Arnaldo began by behaving like normal tourists, visiting the usual sites of national interest. But when they went to Tirana, the capital, they took Arnaldo's guitar with them. An outing to a local park looked innocent enough to anyone in authority who might care to watch. And what harm could there be in two strange foreigners sitting on a park bench, one strumming a guitar and the other, older and wearing glasses, looking at some postcards?

Unable to speak openly to people about Jesus Christ, they had come up with the idea of showing people a selection of English scenic postcards, some of which had churches on them, in the hope that a conversation would start. If it did they would ask if the person knew anything about Easter. Sadly, no one admitted to this. Arnaldo would sing songs with Christian words and personalize them for the Albanians. Michael did discover buildings that had once been churches, but Albanians were no longer allowed to use them for that purpose. Wherever they went, Michael and Arnaldo tried to talk to people about the Lord Jesus. They had managed to take a small radio into the country, intending to pick up programmes beamed at Albania from Christian radio stations in Europe and test the reception. If possible, they would pass on information about frequencies to nationals. They also had a tape recorder and Trans-World Radio had given them gospel tapes in Albanian to play to people they met.

One day, they met a group of students who were willing to talk. One of them, whose name was Ferdinand, actually borrowed the tapes and a copy of Mark's Gospel. Amazingly, he not only listened to them, but also asked if they could give him the recorder, as he wanted to hear more. He wouldn't give them his address, however, because he lived with his parents and didn't want to get into trouble. But he showed them a bus stop, which he often used and where, at a certain time, they would all meet. To their dismay, they never found Ferdinand. Michael was particularly sad about this, as at the time the lad had seemed so interested.

In discussions, they would be told, 'We don't believe in God, our leader is Enver Hoxha!' To which Michael would reply, 'We do believe in God, and our leader is Jesus Christ!' Once when they had been speaking to two young men who had argued strongly with them, Michael and Arnaldo discovered that they had been reported to the police. 'Religious propaganda' was the accusation. Although nothing came of it, as there was no proof, the Albanian guide started to make indirect insinuations. Throughout their time in the country they met only one or two Christians. One was a guide, who when they attempted to take his picture, covered his face with his hand. The other worked as a waitress in a restaurant. Michael offered her a New Testament, which she refused, as she was too afraid to take it.

On his return, Michael wrote: 'In every corner of the country you can read these words: "Rrofte shoku Enver Hoxha (Glory to comrade Enver Hoxha)". The pride and self-sufficient attitude of the Albanian people, especially of their leader Hoxha, has gone up to the throne of the Almighty who is even higher than the eagle (Albania is the land of the eagles). Hoxha's days are counted and he will be overthrown by the Lord. Then, we believe that the gospel will go through again in that country in a new and fresh spiritual life as in Paul's times, when he preached in ancient Illyricum (which is the modern Albania).'

Ten years later, a lady from Lancashire was working in Italy among a group of Albanians. A man came up to her and asked, 'I don't suppose you know a man called Michael Pollard? He has a friend called Arnaldo.'

'Well yes, actually it just so happens that I do!' she replied, 'In fact, I know both of them.'

It was Ferdinand. Unbeknown to Michael and Arnaldo, after their departure from Albania, Ferdinand had returned to his home, where he read Mark's Gospel several times. He was so afraid of being found with it in his possession that he tore it up into little pieces, making sure that he got rid of the evidence without anyone knowing. If the authorities had caught him with it he could have been killed. Such was the fear in that atheistic state that people with biblical names had to change them, for fear of reprisals. It was reported that some priests had been put into barrels with spikes in them and then put into the water to drown. It was extremely dangerous for anyone to show any outward profession of faith. Within a very short time after destroying the booklet, Ferdinand was visited by the secret police. They interrogated him at home, but found no incriminating evidence. Apparently, he had been reported to them because he had been seen talking to foreigners. He was taken to the police headquarters and interrogated for a whole week but then released.

By this time Ferdinand had made a life-changing choice. After reading about Jesus Christ for the first time in Mark's Gospel, he repented of his sins and trusted Jesus as his Lord and Saviour, believing that he was and is God.

Another crack had appeared in the foundations of the atheistic state.

The rat-catcher

Simon and Anna were two Romanian Christians, who were regularly harassed by the authorities, and had been sentenced to a number of years in prison. Anna was painfully crippled with a debilitating arthritic condition. This had been brought on by terrible cruelty by the prison guards and also the awful conditions in which she was kept. The cell where Simon was placed was next to that of a Romanian pastor, Richard Wurmbrand, who used Morse code to communicate with his fellow prisoners through the thick walls. In this way he was able to encourage the other inmates and led not a few to faith in Christ. Wurmbrand's ingenuity and persistence were typical of many Christians in Eastern Europe. Simon himself demonstrated a similar spirit.

Some years later, when Simon and Anna had been released from custody, we discovered that Simon had been banned from preaching by the Communist government. No longer able to function as a pastor with a congregation who came to him, Simon would go walking in the hills, far from the prying eyes of the government officials. He would invite various students to come with him 'to get some exercise'. As they walked kilometre after kilometre they would discuss questions about God and the Bible. Later these students were to become Christian leaders in different parts of the country.

No longer a pastor, Simon needed some sort of employment, so the government made him a rat-catcher, no doubt seeing this as a way to humiliate him. Once again, Simon managed to turn his unfortunate circumstances into opportunities to serve God. In those days travel was neither easy nor cheap but he was able to use his official rail pass to travel far and wide. By day, he caught and disposed of the rats in the numerous villages he visited. But by night he would take a Bible study in a home or conduct a service for villagers. In these areas many people had no transport or else lived far from a church, so, knowing their desire to learn about him, the God who doesn't make mistakes sent them a preacher - and funded his work through the Communist Party! Not for the first time, it seemed as though God had a sense of humour.

The invisible family

Today Kosova is well known as the scene of multiple tragedies. Many nations around the world have become involved with peacekeeping efforts, bringing the area to our attention and on to our television screens. Our involvement in Pec, Kosova, goes back many years.

On one journey, a publisher from Novi-sad had given us Christian books to deliver to a family who had many problems to cope with, including opposition from the hierarchy of the Orthodox Church. This was in the 'difficult' days and in an area where most of the inhabitants were Muslims. Our friend was a Baptist pastor and life was certainly not easy for him and his family. We spent an enjoyable time with them but all too soon it was time to move on. They needed to get to Greece where they were to attend a youth camp; it was impossible to have such camps in Yugoslavia during the days of Communism. They asked if they might travel with us. We piled into our camper van and set off together. I remember all too well how hot it felt in the vehicle with the extra luggage and bodies! Despite the cramped conditions, we made the best of it and enjoyed being together as Christians, talking and laughing. Inevitably, the police flagged us down - a much more scary experience in Communist countries than in Great Britain or New Zealand. The fact that they wanted to see our documents and check the contents of the van was neither surprising nor unusual; we had undergone this many times before and had expected it to happen at some stage. What made things different this time was that the van contained five extra people plus their luggage. How could we explain that to the police? We could be in big trouble - and our friends too. Hearts were beating very fast as we prayed silently. How we needed God's help!

The officials demanded to see our passports and vehicle documents. Then, to our horror, they insisted on inspecting the living area of the van. This was where our friends were sitting - each clutching their passports and personal papers. The police gave no more than a cursory glance round the van and returned our documents - while completely ignoring our passengers. They thanked us for our co-operation and, satisfied, drove off to find their next foreigners.

At first we couldn't understand why the family hadn't been questioned, but then we realized that if God could make blind eyes see, then surely he could make seeing eyes blind. The explanation of the mystery was simple: those policemen couldn't see the family at all!

The second pair of glasses

'I've a terrible headache! Where's the paracetamol?' Who hasn't said this at some time? Of course, in the West most homes have some tablets at hand in the medicine cupboard, and every chemist and supermarket has plentiful supplies. Even if you have a serious disease that requires you to take tablets daily for the rest of your life, prescriptions are available and free if you are over sixty-five years of age or exempt for some other reason. When there is a charge, it is often less than the real cost of the medicine. But for our friends behind the Iron Curtain, it was a very different situation. During the seventies, many Christians in Eastern Europe had difficulty in obtaining medication. So we regularly took supplies for the young and old, as well as trying to help with more unusual requests. 'Jan', our friend in Bulgaria, was the pastor of a local church. A quiet man who lived alone, he had for a number of years been targeted by the police and was consequently frightened and lonely. He also suffered from Parkinson's disease and was unable to get the medication he urgently needed. Every time we visited him we took a prescription which would cover his needs for a year. It was impossible to post the medicine to him, because it would be stolen or confiscated. One year he asked if we could also get an optician to make up his prescription for new glasses, which was not possible in his town. We did so and packed them carefully, sending them by recorded delivery.

Jan answered the door one day to see the postman on his doorstep. 'Your glasses from England have arrived,' the man told him. You can imagine Jan's joy; he would be able to read again. But he had not taken account of the Bulgarian secret police. 'Unfortunately,' the postman continued, 'you can't have them because you are a Christian.' He turned and left, taking the glasses with him. Jan was devastated.

Some months later, Michael was off school with a back problem. He decided to tidy one of the drawers by his bed and - lo and behold - there was Jan's prescription! We decided to get another pair of glasses for him and since at my school there was a young lad whose parents were going to travel through Bulgaria, I wondered if they might be able to post the glasses for Jan while they were over there. They were happy to oblige but in the end the Bulgarian student, who was working there as a guide, said she thought it would be better if she delivered the glasses personally. That would ensure their arrival at the right address for the correct recipient. She was as good as her word. Our friend was thrilled to bits that he was able to read again.

The body that moved the clothes

Basingstoke may seem an unlikely place for a miracle to begin. But in the event there were two.

'Would you take an iron and kettle to someone in Romania, please?' We were more than happy to respond to this innocent request. Unfortunately, the delivery was made only a few days before we were due to set off. Michael and I didn't finish working until the day before our departure, so time was at a premium and there was so much to pack, sort out and plan. Imagine our surprise and dismay when there was no kettle, no iron - just six or seven bags of clothes.

Our test has always been, 'If you or your children can't wear it for best, then don't give it to us!' But when we looked at the bags, not only had several of them split but they were spilling out garments that were discarded and old, worthy, we thought, to be described as 'rubbish'. However, as the old lady in Romania had been promised them, we felt obliged to take the lot even if they were neither an iron nor a kettle. This was a dilemma we didn't want to repeat and we reminded ourselves that in future we must check any 'gifts' beforehand.

First we headed for Hungary to visit friends, before going to many drop-off points with book-aid deliveries. Our friends had given us the address of some Hungarians who regularly visited relatives in Romania in exactly the same area that our 'big-bag clothes delivery' was destined for. 'Before the changes' (the common name for the old Communist days), it was a great help to know 'someone' who knew 'somebody' who could put us in touch with a 'person' . . . Often we could not write down names and addresses for fear of being searched and implicating our friends. We had to memorize many strange-sounding places and personal names, occasionally resorting to invisible ink if our brain cells were not functioning accurately.

Having made it to the next couple, we were relieved to hear them say that they would gladly do the last leg of the journey themselves and deliver the clothes to the lady in Romania next time they were free to go there. They were a delightful couple and typically hospitable in providing ample refreshment for us. But all was not well with our vehicle. It was in its death throes and the various rumbling and creaks from the engine and chassis were its last gasps. Eventually it decided enough was enough and promptly gave up the ghost. Feeling rather like naughty children in disgrace, we were ignominiously towed out of Hungary and pushed into Austria. The van was abandoned in a burial place for dead and dying vehicles. The AA provided us with a small car, enabling us to make it back to Rotterdam where we caught the ferry to England.

Meanwhile, back at the Hungarian border, our intrepid friends, Mr and Mrs Rottmiyer, tried to enter Romania with their six bags of clothes. The border guards gave them a hard time. 'Yes, you can enter,' they were told, 'but you will have to pay duty on the clothes.' The Rottmiyers definitely did not have the kind of money that was demanded - the equivalent of £250-£300. So they left the clothes there, visited their relatives and picked the clothes up again when they passed through customs on their way home. This exercise was repeated several times. Then God took over.

Mrs Rottmiyer's brother came to stay with them for a holiday. Sadly, he became ill and passed away and arrangements were quickly made to return his body to Romania. Then, as they were packing the car, the couple suddenly had a bright idea. First they loaded in the by now famous - or infamous - bags of clothes, then carefully placed the corpse on top of them. They reached the border. The guards took one look at the macabre contents and hastily waved them through! I doubt if the recipient of the clothes was immensely grateful for the motley collection of garments, but we had eventually kept our promise, something we always tried to do!

All the same, we had a problem. We had made it safely back home, but we were without a vehicle. Quickly we began to search for another camper van. Or should it have been - a hearse?

The gardener's return

Karl-Marx-Stadt was a large city in East Germany (now known as Chemnitz). We had met our friend 'Maria' at the Baptist Church there, where she was the caretaker. Her husband 'Franz' was German but she was from Estonia. The Communist regime made it extremely difficult for her to return to her country, but she would faithfully scrape and save from her meagre earnings so that she could travel back home from time to time. Once she shared with us in confidence her desire to secretly take with her Bibles in Estonian; but it was virtually impossible to find these anywhere in East Germany. So whenever we visited her we would deliver Bibles, which we had purchased for her in England.

In those days there were various hazards about our trips to Eastern Europe. Often we had no idea how to find our contacts. We could not easily ask for directions, as one never knew whether the person asked was an informer working with the secret police. We had to be very careful so as not to put our Christian friends at risk. Also we were always mindful that our visits had to be with God's timing; this was one of the things we asked many people back home in Shipley and elsewhere to pray about for us. Our contacts might be out of the country or ill or just simply away from home, meaning that we would could not deliver our consignments.

There was another possibility - they could be under surveillance by the secret police.

One year our visit to Maria presented several difficulties. She had moved house; in addition she used to spend long periods away tending a large garden belonging to an elderly couple. They were from her church, but old age and infirmity prevented them from coping with such a large plot. Our friend had written saying that if she wasn't at home we would find her at the garden. We didn't want to make a wasted journey so prayed, 'Please, Lord, help us find the lady in Karl-Marx-Stadt.' Unfortunately our memories of the garden and its location were extremely vague, to say the least. Rather than get lost and waste time looking for a garden, who knows where, we headed for Maria's home. Perhaps a neighbour might know where she was; but in that case we would have to try and find the garden. All this would take up valuable travelling time, besides which, a foreign van driving round, apparently aimlessly, would look highly suspicious to the police.

To our relief, we found the new address in Karl-Marx-Stadt without a hitch. Michael knocked on the door. The door opened . . . and there stood Maria! Welcoming us inside she explained, 'The weather has been so good, we have been staying at the garden for the last week. I had no intentions of coming home today. But while I was working in the garden, I felt the overwhelming desire to come back - there was no reason to return, we had everything we wanted, but yet, deep inside, I felt there was something important! Now I know that if I hadn't obeyed, we would have missed each other.' The consignment of Estonian Bibles was safely deposited where prying eyes could not see them, before beginning the next leg of their journey to Russia. And for us? Back on the road for our next delivery.

The needle in the haystack

'We want you to buy a horse. Well, not you personally, but a family in the Ukraine needs one. Could you take some money to them? They are terribly poor but if they could buy a horse they could farm more efficiently. It would really help them to survive.'

We were more than happy to oblige these generous benefactors and with our vehicle full of the usual load of 'goodies' we set off to cross Europe. There was a problem, however. Somehow we had lost the address! It helped that we knew the area roughly; the nearest city was Rovno. But we had never been there before and Rovno is a big city with a large population. Obviously, the farm would be in the countryside, but in which direction? All we had was a photograph of the family.

Our arrival in the Ukraine was spectacular. While we were debating how on earth we would ever be able to find the family, our vehicle came to a sudden and soggy stop. An important hose had split and water was pouring out in a continuous stream. We were in a real mess. It looked as if we were definitely not going anywhere. What were we going to do? At home we could just phone the recovery service, who would probably get us back on the road again within an hour - but the Ukraine was slightly different!

However, as if on cue, a car happened to pull up alongside of us. The driver got out and offered to help. He even spoke a little English. He peered under the bonnet and extracted the offending hose. 'Stay here,' he said, 'I'll be back soon.' We didn't have much choice, so we were relieved when some time later he returned. He had managed to create a good hose by joining another piece of rubber to our old bit. We thanked him profusely as he returned to his car. (I hoped he understood my feeble attempts to thank him in Ukrainian.) Then, as he was getting in, I heard him say something. I turned to Michael and said, 'I'm sure that man has just said to us "God bless you" in Ukrainian!'

Michael took the photograph to our 'Good Samaritan' and asked, 'Do you know this family?' The man smiled as he pointed at one of the sons. 'He is my best friend!' He was able to give us the address plus clear instructions as to how to find the farm. We arrived safely the following morning and delivered the money, which was gratefully received. It was yet another answer to our prayers.

God promises to lead and guide us.

Babies and false teeth

Not every trip was 'plain sailing'. In August 1983 we were turned away from the Romanian border because we had a huge amount of clothing, which we had been asked to take for an old lady. The customs officers were adamant that we could not deliver the clothing. They were also not impressed when they found some syringes and spatulas, which we were taking to a hospital in Iasi, in the north of Romania. The medical goods were confiscated and we drove reluctantly away from the country we loved so dearly, and which was in so much need of help. We decided to go to Hungary, to visit some friends who we hadn't seen for several years. We made our way to their home and rang the door bell with hope and expectation. To our pleasure and relief our friend Ildiko came to the door with a new baby in her arms. I just love babies and my heart went out to this lovely young mother. I asked her, 'Is there anything you need for the baby, just tell us and you can have whatever you want.'

Imagine the shock Michael and I had as both husband and wife burst into tears. I thought I must have upset them. I felt awful. I was at a loss what to say or do. But then came the explanation. Geza had lost his job. The reason was simple; he had been leading Bible studies for students at Budapest University. These kinds of things happened often under strict Communist regimes. Then Ildiko and Geza discovered they were going to have a third child. With no wage coming in, they didn't have the money to buy the things they needed for their tiny baby. That very morning they had been on their knees asking the Lord to help them to feed and clothe their baby. They trusted their Lord completely but they hadn't expected the answer to come so soon!

Among Michael's favourite Bible verses were Isaiah 55:8 and 9: 'My thoughts are not your thoughts, nor are your ways my ways', says the Lord. 'For as the heavens are higher than the earth, so are my ways higher than your ways and my thoughts than your thoughts.' Suddenly, Michael and I began to realize why we had been prevented from going to Romania. It is always exciting to see answers to prayer, but even better to be an answer to prayer!

While Ildiko was seeing to the baby, her husband was happily talking to us. All at once, he stopped in mid-sentence, putting his hand to his mouth. He was obviously very embarrassed. Geza apologized profusely for the state of his teeth. Only the day before, the dentist had told him that all his badly discoloured teeth needed to be extracted. 'I must get a job before I can have them seen to,' he explained, sadly. While Geza was helping Ildiko, Michael and I looked at each other. Before we left home, the Pastor of Tinshill Free Church in Leeds had given us an envelope containing some money. He had said that the Lord would show us who to give it to. We had both thought it would be for someone in Romania, but we had been prevented from going there. Now we felt that this was the man to whom we should give the envelope. So when Geza returned we lovingly gave it to him. Carefully folding back the paper Geza looked inside. Tears began to roll down his cheeks. The amount in the envelope was the exact price he had been quoted by the dentist the day before.

Poland

The Polish language is one of the most difficult languages to get one's tongue around. Fortunately Michael had to find his way not only to places such as Swinoujscie (Swin oo oo shyuh, or something similar) but also to the simpler-sounding Sopot and Gdansk. The latter was making headlines in our newspapers when the men of the shipyards came to the fore by demonstrating about conditions and the political situation in Poland. Lech Walensa was the spokesperson who went on to win political status in his country. Poland's recovery from being (mostly) flattened during the Second World War was hampered to some extent by the 'claws' of Communism. Economic growth was restricted until political change released the claws, which however were replaced by the 'tentacles' of the materialistic West, bringing both the good and bad features of democratic freedom. All the same, to the humble traveller and tourist in the seventies and eighties, entering Poland was a welcome relief from the fierce interrogation by the security guards of its neighbours, particularly East Germany.

During our summer trips, the hot sun would bathe the many cornfields with nature's pure gold. On closer inspection the swatches of red among the corn revealed themselves as hosts of wild poppies fluttering exuberantly in the breeze, nestling comfortably with white daises and soft blue cornflowers. The drone of combine harvesters could be heard as they worked in tandem bringing in the precious harvest. God himself had indeed touched the landscape of Poland with his creatorial paint box, for there was a myriad of flowers in gardens and out-of-the-way places.

All this, we noticed, was in sharp contrast to Holland, whose horticulturists maintain the fields in pristine full-growth condition: weed-free, stuffed and saturated with fertilizer. As we travelled east, the fields became increasingly dominated by weeds, producing a much weaker crop. Everywhere houses were in various states of construction or repair. Nothing ever seemed to be completed. The concrete blocks of flats in towns and cities and the buildings everywhere were crying out for coloured paint. Often we could see only one dim light bulb lighting the whole interior - no light shades. The colour of Communism was definitely grey!

The washing machine and the fatted calf

On our first visit to Poland we had been given the address of a young man who was studying at a Bible college in Warsaw. His future wife was living with her mother in a small village in the south of Poland. It was a mainly Russian-speaking area, close to the border with Belarus. The cottage had an earthen floor, with rugs, made from rags, scattered about the tiny room. The kitchen held a soot-blackened stove that provided warmth in the cold winters and too much heat in the summer. One room was set apart, to be used as a 'church' on Sundays.

Rebecca, our elder daughter, was a toddler when she first visited Poland and we had decided not to give her the local food or milk. Like all travellers with small children, we had to be careful about food and hygiene. There were occasions when it would have been impolite to refuse our very generous hosts, but happily she survived and so did we. However, we did worry about germs and infections, as we, unlike our friends, hadn't built up any immunity to local 'bugs'. In the event of an emergency, the well-equipped hospitals of West Germany were a long way off. Despite our grumbles about waiting times at clinics and accident and emergency centres, we realized that we had a lot to be thankful for, especially our National Health Service.

Imagine having no running water, let alone a choice between hot or cold. Every day, water had to be pulled up out of a well by the hen house in the garden. We left Olga and her mother with Christian literature and Polish Bibles and provided them with clothing, food items and medical supplies, such as we would have in our medicine chest at home. They had so little, but never complained about their poverty, knowing that they had a loving Father, able to supply their every need. The couple married and over the years we continued visiting Olga and Anatol and their family. They bought some land and built a new, larger wooden house. In the middle of the house was a small chapel that was used by the Polish-speaking Baptists in the vicinity. Most of the churches in that area were Russian-speaking and much larger in numbers.

One year when we went to visit Anatol and Olga we discovered that they had managed to scrimp and save enough money to buy a washing machine. Previously they had no electricity and their water had to be pumped from the well. Anatol, like many Eastern

Europeans, managed to install the electricity and plumbed in the water himself. Olga was very happy and proud of her practical husband. 'Would you like to use the washing machine?' Olga asked. We had three children and were living in cramped conditions in the camper van throughout the summer, so this was an offer I could not refuse. When I had finished, Anatol asked Michael to help him carry the precious washing machine outside. Michael was somewhat worried by this request. 'Have we damaged the machine?'

'Oh no, not at all,' Anatol assured him. Together they lifted the precious washing machine up on to their very old vehicle in the yard. Innocently, we asked Anatol what he was doing. 'Today I am going to Belarus to some people who are very poor. They could never afford to buy a washing machine so we are going to give them ours.' I felt so guilty as I knew that I could not ever think of giving away my own washing machine. Would we be prepared to give in such a sacrificial way?

We thanked them for their hospitality as they drove off toward the Russian border. As we made our way towards Warsaw, we spoke of the love and generosity we had seen demonstrated by people who themselves had few of this world's goods and without a second thought were prepared to give away something special.

It was some years later before we met again and I was desperate to discover what had happened to the washing machine. Anatol looked quite sad as he described how when they arrived at the border the customs officers would not allow them to take the washing machine into Belarus and so it was theirs to take home. It reminded me of the story in Genesis 22 where God tells Abraham to sacrifice his son Isaac. Abraham was prepared to obey God, but as he was about to strike the fatal blow, God honoured his faith and Abraham saw a ram, which he was told to sacrifice instead of his son. A son is infinitely more precious than a washing machine - but God honoured Anatol's faith, as he did that of Abraham.

With the new house came quite a large amount of land, which the family has utilized. They grow most of their vegetables and fruit and preserve much of their harvest for the bitter winters. They have hens, ducks, geese, cows and sheep, which will most likely end up in the cooking pot. The last time Michael and I went to see the family we enjoyed our usual tour all round the farm, followed by some of the animals who were curious to see what we were up to and probably hoping for food. Our vehicle was on the drive and next to the passenger door was a fence where Olga had hung a carpet she had washed, to let it dry in the sun. *Dry* it would be, but clean, probably not. Not because Olga had neglected her duties, but because a gaggle of geese had decided to perch on the carpet, from where they could get a bird's-eye view of the interior of our vehicle and some of the contents! As their confidence grew, they flew in and made themselves at home, returning after they had been evicted.

We watched Olga as she hand-milked the cows with the young calf nestling beside. It left us with a happy memory, but not for long! We went to visit some other Christian friends who lived quite near and promised to pop in and see Anatol and Olga again on the Sunday before we set off for home. When we arrived back at their home on the Sunday, Anatol and Olga generously insisted that we had something to eat, even though we were going back for Sunday dinner with our other friends. To our consternation, we were given soup containing some of the remains of the calf we had been watching and enjoying just two days earlier! It was an overwhelming experience but one which we would not have minded missing. Obviously, the calf would provide meat for the winter, but I just wished that they had needed it for milk rather than meat!

After Michael's death, money from the Family Fund set up in his memory was sent to help increase Anatol's flock of sheep and herd of cows, so that they are able to sell the milk, meat and wool and give the family a well-deserved income.

The woman struck by lightning

What on earth could connect Quito in Ecuador and a doctor in England with a severe storm in Poland? The answer is - a radio!

One summer we were packing up the vehicle as usual with food, Bibles and medicines, this time to take to Poland. Our local doctor, who knew about our travels, offered us a very fine new radio. 'Do you know of anyone who could use it?' he said. 'I too am a Christian, I have contacts with a radio station in Quito, Ecuador, which is where I got this radio. Perhaps somebody would be able to use it to tune into Christian programmes?' Gratefully, we replied, 'We don't know of anyone in particular, but we'll pray about it and God will guide us to the right person.'

It was our third visit to Poland. We had friends in Bydgoszcz, including Jan, the pastor of the evangelical church, who was involved in youth camps in the 'Lake District' of Poland. God had marvellously provided a large lakeside building, which was the venue for wonderful holidays during the summer, giving time for Bible study by various groups, including the disabled. We asked Jan if he knew someone who would like a radio.

Yes, he thought he knew just the right person. Tucked away in a small village was a very poor lady. Her possessions were few, but she did have a radio. Each day she listened to all sorts of programmes. One day as she twiddled the dials, she discovered a Christian programme. She carefully took in what she had heard - how she could come to know God for herself, how Jesus died for her sins, rose from the dead and could give forgiveness for sins, peace and power to live life day by day and eventually a home in heaven. There at home, sitting by her radio, she was converted. She was so excited - immediately she told her family and friends about what had happened. She wanted them to become Christians too! But their reactions were different from hers. Some told her she was out of her mind. Some just ignored her.

But she continued to grow spiritually as a Christian. She was not a well woman. She had a serious heart complaint but expensive, 'state of the art' medical know-how and technology were well out of her reach. Her living conditions were very basic and difficult. One night, as she was praying, she asked the Lord why she had to live in such a hovel. That night her home was struck by lightning and the contents destroyed. Her beloved radio was gone. Not only that, however, something else had gone. As the house was struck by lightning, the shock resolved her heart problem. The other villagers helped to rebuild her home, replacing the old hovel. Many people became Christians because of her testimony. And what joy she had when a brand new radio was delivered to her! Now she could share the Christian programmes with others in the village. Prayer certainly does change things.

Bulgaria

Bulgaria was among the most loyal Balkan allies of the Soviet Union and also probably one of the least known of the Eastern European countries. Although it had - and still has - a tourist trade, this wasn't promoted in the West. Bulgaria was beset by currency regulations and border regulations - all over the place, in fact, there were regulations and restrictions, so much beloved by the Communist regimes. During the final years of the last century, political changes brought a move towards democracy but without the full glare of the Western press. This meant that the change was less of an upheaval for the people but the shift from full employment and job security to capitalism's free market economy didn't enthuse everyone.

Some know Bulgaria for its wines, some for its package holidays, but I remember it for the people and for our Bulgarian adventures. I remember one man in particular, who translated Christian literature from English into Bulgarian, as government restrictions meant that such books could not be obtained from bookshops. His eyesight was almost non-existent and I'll never understand how he managed to complete such daunting tasks. He supplemented his thick spectacle lenses by using an enormous magnifying glass. I wonder if the people who benefited from his work ever knew what personal cost lay behind those books.

The non-existent church

At least fourteen vehicles were queuing at the border inspection point. We were praying hard that our special cargo would get through safely. On one side of the crossing a Yugoslav guard was listening to a football match. Then, just before our van was due to be inspected, Yugoslavia scored. The man listening to the radio rushed out to tell his comrades. They were so delighted that they let the van go through without inspecting it. Not for the first time we were glad for football matches, especially when making those all-important border crossings.

It was in the early seventies that we first visited Bulgaria, taking Bibles and Christian literature with us. We had been told that in Burgas there was a Christian working in the travel bureau who spoke English. So we decided to go there to contact him, hoping he would advise us as to whom we should give the Bibles. But although we found the travel bureau, we didn't find the man. Michael, ever optimistic, asked the assistant if he could tell us where we could find a church. He didn't know, but made a phone call, then passed the phone to Michael. 'There are no churches in Bulgaria, and no one believes in God. There is no God', shouted an angry voice at on the other end of the phone Then it was slammed down.

We continued exploring the city and found a folk-dance club in a building which had previously had been a church. Then, just as we were ready to give up, we saw a Catholic church and left a few Bibles where they would be found. As we came out, we saw the caretaker about to lock the doors. We asked if he knew where we could find the Baptist church. His face beamed. We learned that there was one church, which was Pentecostal. In those days only one Protestant church was allowed in a town as a rule, so Christians of different denominations gathered together. We arrived at the church just two minutes before the service was due to begin. Afterwards we spoke to some Swedish folk who spoke English and were obviously known and trusted by the pastor. We told them we had Christian literature and Bibles with us and would give them to the pastor if he wanted them. Michael and I went to collect them, but there was a slight hitch - we couldn't remember where we had parked the car! It took us a long time to locate it, but about midnight we were back at the church with our contraband. Someone was waiting in the darkness and quickly and quietly we handed the things over with no word spoken and no names given.

Escape from the KGB

'The cruelty of atheism is hard to believe,' writes Richard Wurmbrand, who certainly knows what he's talking about. 'When man has no faith in the reward of good or the punishment of evil, there is no reason to be human. . . .When a member of the Underground Church is arrested, a terrible drama strikes his family. It is highly illegal for anyone to help them. His family suffers endlessly. I can tell for a fact, that if rank-and-file Christians in the free world had not sent me and my family help, we would never have survived and lived to be with you and write these words![5] As Wurmbrand points out, his experience was not unique. Another pastor who suffered for his faith was Georgi Vins, a Reform Baptist pastor from the Soviet Union. In January 1975 he was sentenced in Kiev to five years' imprisonment followed by five years' exile, having been found guilty of 'damaging the interests of citizens under the pretext of religious activity'. For forty-five years, three generations, the Vins family suffered bitter persecution for their faith.

For us, chattering monkeys and roaring lions provided the perfect background for a day out with friends at the city zoo. None of us was a spy or guilty of espionage, criminal activity, or treason. But all the same we knew that careless conversations could get our contacts and us into serious trouble. Our 'crime'? Simply that of being Christians. So we just mingled with the crowd and no one gave us a second look. It was good to talk together about the problems experienced by Christians in the Ukraine. We discovered what their needs were and how we could help them. We were able to relax with them and get to know them in a deeper way. Before we left, we were given directions about how to get to the church the next day. We were really looking forward to seeing our friends again.

Unfortunately, Rebecca was unwell in the morning, so I stayed behind to look after her. Michael made his way there on his own. The church was in a large house, which had been adapted for use as a place of worship. Before the service began, the large choir was singing. Michael asked permission to take some photographs and was told to take them from the choir seats. But when he returned downstairs he was approached by a man who demanded his passport and camera. Michael had already put these out of the way in a pocket. And as a group of people realized that the secret police were trying to arrest Michael for taking the photographs, they gathered so tightly round the man that he couldn't move.

A friend led Michael to a small room where they both jumped out of the window. They ran to the bottom of the garden, climbed on the roof of a dog kennel and then leaped on to the railway line. They kept running and running, not knowing if anyone was following them. When they came to a road they walked along it until they reached a bus stop. A bus came, Michael's helper paid the fare for both of them, then, bending over, whispered the directions for Michael to make his way back to our vehicle. He got off the bus a few stops before Michael, who arrived back at our van, completely exhausted. Quickly we off-loaded the goods, which were to be delivered to the family of Pastor Georgi Vins. Then we left Kiev as fast as we could.

The Russian hymn book and the Mongolian connection

Not many people in the West got to be a guest of the Soviet Union. But Michael did!

My quiet, unassuming husband had been invited to be the guest of the Communist youth movement, the Young Pioneers. One October half-term Michael set off for Russia together with other teachers from Britain. Each day they visited different schools and other educational establishments, including places of culture in Moscow, Leningrad and Riga. In the evenings, the rest of the party would venture out into the city to enjoy the night life. Michael, however, would be off trying to contact Christians.

He found the main Baptist Church in Moscow, where he would sit and listen to their choir practices. When everything was finished, he would say 'goodnight' to each choir member, hoping that one of them could speak English. But alas, not one person could converse with him. One night, as he was going downstairs, he heard voices from below. There at the bottom of the stairs was a small group of men and one woman. One of them who, like Michael, could speak some German, explained that there had just been a delivery of Bibles from the Bible Society and people had come from different parts of the Soviet Union to collect their consignments. Michael shared a time of fellowship with them and one man gave him a Russian hymnbook. Knowing that hymn books were few and far between in Russia, Michael was reluctant to accept the book; he couldn't read the Cyrillic script and in any case singing was not his strong point. But the man insisted that Michael must have it, so he brought it home.

Some years later, when Michael was at a prayer meeting for Mongolia in Bradford, there was an announcement. Someone in Mongolia had sent an urgent request for a Russian hymnbook. As Michael was talking with the others afterwards, he suddenly remembered the book he had been given in Moscow. Where was it now?

Then he remembered that it was safely stowed in one of his drawers in our bedroom - but not for much longer! Soon it was on its way to the church in Mongolia, where copies would be made for their congregation.

Now Michael understood why he had to accept the unexpected hymnbook.

Genovieva

It was the end of a busy day in a school in Romania. The pupils were weary but anxiously awaited the results of their examination. 'Pavel' the teacher began, ' . . . quite good but there were a few mistakes, there is room for improvement; even so you got eight.'

'Carmen, very good, apart from two small mistakes, a ten for you, well done.'

When she reached Genovieva the teacher congratulated her. 'Genovieva, you did very well too, there are no mistakes.' Then she continued, 'You got five - and you know why.'

'It's because she's a Christian', whispers one of the class.

The authorities had instructed teachers to tell the children that God did not exist. If they had Christian pupils, they were to give them bad marks, humiliate them, ridicule them, punish them in front of the whole class, and never give a prize to a child from a Christian family even if they deserved it. Later, when we got to know Genovieva and her family, we were very challenged as we heard how children from Christian homes had been objects of persecution in school. Some were spat on, others had their hair pulled and some were made to kneel on hard dried cobs of corn to humiliate them.

Genovieva was the kind of pupil the authorities had in their sights. Her Christian parents taught her and the rest of the family in the home by example and from the Bible, despite persecution from the authorities. When she began her studies at the university Genovieva had to be careful what she said for one of her friends was Vanda, the daughter of the chief of the secret police. Genovieva was an excellent student of English and one day her pastor asked her to translate for a Danish missionary who was visiting Romania. She hesitated at first as, if Vanda's father found out, she could be expelled from the university. This assignment turned out to be the greatest encounter of her life, for as she translated the gospel message for others, she herself was totally changed by what she heard, making her own personal commitment to Christ there and then, fully aware that this would cost her dearly.

Genovieva's personal faith in God led to her being expelled from university, arrested by the Securitate (the cruel secret police) and imprisoned, through deception, in a mental hospital. For seven years she had a secret 'home' in a church where she worked as a cleaner. Her bed was a bench with a tablecloth as a blanket. Sometimes, she once told me, she had slept in the baptismal tank - although without the water - when she sensed the secret police were searching for her. She lived like this for seven years, but God had a work for her to do for him despite Ceausescu's cruel regime. Using her musical talents she formed a Christian children's choir, distributed Bibles 'smuggled' into the country and eventually, after the revolution, opened a children's home in Iasi. She is an incredibly brave person, full of the joy of the Lord.

As Christians, Genovieva's family faced many problems. Probably the worst time was when her brother was accused of the attempted murder of a policeman. He had borrowed a car from his pastor to take Bibles to a safe hiding place. The one thing they all dreaded eventually happened. In those days just a knock on the door could send shivers of fear up one's spine. Was it a friend or the police? This time it was the Securitate. He was taken to the prison just around the corner from his home. The guards tortured him terribly, beating him with cudgels on the soles of his feet and his stomach. He was drugged and suspended by his wrists from a great height. He was originally sentenced to seven and a half years imprisonment, but was released exactly one year after his arrest. George Shultz, who was the US Secretary of State at that time, personally met with Ceausescu and appealed for his release. The case received much publicity in the West. Many people prayed for Costica. In September 1986, he and his family were allowed to leave Romania and emigrated to the USA.

We were introduced to Genovieva through Simon and Anna. She and her family lived in an impoverished part of northern Romania which was not visited by many travellers from the West. The whole family were thrilled to see us. It was a real privilege to spend time with them. The goods that had been donated to us back home were greatly appreciated by the Romanians. Seeing how little they had, made us wish we could have done more for them.

The man in black

We were with Genovieva when we met the man in black. It was a normal trip to Romania and we were carrying the usual items, children's clothes, things for babies, screw-in light bulbs, food, medicines, prescriptions, toiletries and, of course, Christian literature and Bibles. This particular year we had a large-print Bible for an old lady who lived in a small room in the home of some our friends. She had problems with her eyes, so needed a copy she could read without difficulty.

On our way across Europe, before going to see some other friends, we stopped at a local beauty spot with Genovieva. Suddenly a man dressed in black slipped out of the woods. Genovieva went to speak to him, whilst we enjoyed the scenery. After a while she came to ask if we had a large-print Bible with us, because the man was one of the many Orthodox but evangelical priests, who had been expelled from the church. He was living in the woods, subsisting on whatever berries and plants he could find. He was desperate to have a Bible as his had been confiscated but his eyesight had deteriorated so he needed one with large print. We were in a dilemma. We had promised to take just such a Bible to the old lady. Whose need was the greater? We discussed and prayed for guidance and concluded we should give it to the priest. He was so happy to have the Word of God after so long.

On our way to our next port of call, we popped in to see a Romanian friend for a short time. We told him about the hermit and the Bible, mentioning that the copy we gave him had been intended for an old lady. Our friend climbed on to a chair and lifted up part of the ceiling, put his hand in and brought out a large-print Bible!

We remembered one of the titles given to God in the Old Testament. 'Jehovah Jireh' means 'The Lord will provide.'

Held hostage

God reassured the prophet Jeremiah by telling him, 'I know the plans I have for you, plans to prosper you and not harm you, plans to give you hope and a future.' I think of that when I recall the time when I became a hostage. Border crossing points were quite scary places. No one ever smiled. Suspicion hung in the air waiting the moment to envelop a victim in its ugly garment of intimidation. The guards mistrusted the travellers. The travellers mistrusted the guards. That at any rate was something that both shared. It felt as though some strange complicated political game was being played, with people, fear and persecution being used as dice and counters. Because of our frequent visits, we soon came to recognize certain officials. Some, we knew, were definitely in the category of 'Dangerous - avoid if at all possible!' At the top of that list was Eva, one of the senior border guards on the Romanian frontier. She was fairly thin with blonde hair and a hard face. You might imagine that her favourite drink was vinegar.

One day we arrived at the Romanian border at Varsand. As usual, there was a long line of traffic. There was nothing else to do except turn off the engine and wait for ever - at least that's what it seemed like. The children waited too. These times really tested everyone's patience; sometimes, if we were going through a particularly sensitive area, we would give them long-lasting sweets that took a lot of sucking and chewing, thus making sure that they wouldn't come out with any remarks that could get us into trouble.

Nervously we watched the custom officers checking the vehicles ahead of us. Those from the West were separated from those from the Socialist countries. Inspection of the latter was rapid and far from thorough; they made it through to the Hungarian side very quickly. Meanwhile, the rest of us were waiting, frustrated by the slowness of it all. We were the last in the queue and had no choice but to endure the long wait and watch the proceedings. These guards undoubtedly deserved a prize for thoroughness! They were removing absolutely everything from the vehicles. Some items were simply confiscated. If they found letters that were to be posted in the West they tore them into shreds and binned them. Michael and I were glad there was nothing in our vehicle that would cause problems; on the other hand, ours was much larger than the others and would take ages to check.

There was a woman on duty, which probably meant trouble, for in our experience the women guards were generally far worse than the men. But this was not just any woman. It was Eva. So we knew we were in for a hard time. As always, we prayed that God would guide us though all circumstances. Back home, friends too would be asking God to help us. Eva went to Michael's side of the van. We were ready for her; trusting that somehow our responses might be the right ones. If not, she might keep us there for hours. Just then, as if on cue, Eva put her hand to her head as if she had a terrible headache. Without a word she made her way to the customs building and never returned. One big obstacle had been removed but we still had the problem of going through customs. However, the officer who replaced Eva gave us only a cursory inspection. Before we knew it, we were on our way with no problems. In the hour or so that we spent on the Hungarian side of the border, changing money, having our passports and legal documents for the vehicle checked and the van inspected, not one Western vehicle came through the border from Romania.

We didn't see Eva again until 1985 - but that was a different story! Our journey that year had taken us as far as Hungary. A family with whom we had stayed kindly offered hospitality before we crossed the border into Romania for the next leg of our travels. The pastor there had given us some addresses of people in Romania, which were stowed out of sight in the camper van. It was about 4 p.m. when we arrived at the border. Rain was pouring down. Everything seemed miserable and, to add to our discomfort, the electricity was off. Our passports and visas had been taken to be checked but nothing was happening. It was boring. We were all getting fed up with waiting. Our thoughts were focused on the need to hurry on to Romania while there were still some hours left in the day. 'Not much longer!' we told the children. How wrong we were.

At last we were told to move the vehicle to the customs area. The officer on duty was . . . Eva! This time she didn't have a headache but we had no doubt that she was about to give us one. She started to examine our vehicle and asked if we had Bibles. We said 'yes' and showed her our own Bibles. This infuriated her. She called for some male guards to go through the vehicle searching for more Bibles. The search was both relentless and destructive; they ripped the panelling off one side, broke the back step and pulled a metal strip off the back.

They even tried to break into our sixteen-gallon water tank. Michael was taken away to be strip-searched, but a New Testament in his pocket was ignored.

Suddenly I thought of those Romanian addresses. The list could cause a lot of problems for the Romanians whose names were on it, even though they didn't know us and we didn't know them. We usually memorized them but if we had to write them down, we used either a code or invisible ink. I realized I had to get rid of that list. But how, with everybody watching us? I gathered up the night-clothes, toothbrushes, toothpaste, soap, and towels and said that I was going to get the children ready for bed. I found a sanitary towel, made a slit in it and slipped the addresses inside. As we were leaving the vehicle we had to show what we had in our hands. The sanitary towel was scarcely noticed. I took the children with me into the area with toilet facilities. 'Get washed please, all of you,' I ordered, trying to act as normally as possible. My first job was to tear up the addresses and flush them down the loo, but - horror of horrors - all the little bits of paper were floating on the top! I asked Rebecca to go to the loo, but she said, 'I've already been!'

Well, go again, Rebecca and again and again! Flush the water until the little bits of paper have gone!' In those days I would not have been surprised if the guards had collected each piece of paper from the toilet and tried to reconstruct the addresses.

Our next ordeal was a series of demands for money. We were told that because we had been found with Bibles we had to pay a fine of £2,500 or forfeit the vehicle. Michael offered £800 but this was not acceptable. We had quite a lot of money to give to people in need in Romania; but we were not prepared to use it to pay the fine. It had been given in trust for others, so it was not ours to spend. We asked for permission to contact the British embassy in Bucharest, in order to inform them of our situation, to ask for help and legal advice. But though we begged and pleaded with the officials, insisting that it was our right to do this, they continually refused. One person tried to fob us off by saying it wasn't possible to phone to Bucharest from Varsand. However, it had been by telephoning her superior in Bucharest, that Eva was able to determine the consequences of our misdemeanours.

After a good night's sleep in the caravanette, we awoke feeling apprehensive, as the guards made further demands for money. Michael handed over £800, which they took, but they still wanted more. I stayed in the van while Michael and the children went with the guards to the Hungarian side of the border. Michael needed to get in touch with the British embassy to ask them to contact our bank. I stayed behind because I was worried that the men might search our vehicle again and find the money designated for the poor. It was hidden in the gas cooker, along with various cooking items. I had to think of some way of getting the money to Michael without anyone knowing.

I was allowed to pass some basic necessities over to Michael. 'I've got the milk powder, drinking chocolate and matches out of the *gas cooker*. *Everything* is in the bag', I hurriedly told him, hoping he would comprehend my cryptic message. Would he understand that I meant the money for Romania? Fortunately he did.

I sat waiting, fully expecting the others to return. What a shock it was when the guards told me that I was a 'voluntary hostage'! I watched the family walk away, each followed by an armed escort pushing a rifle in their back. After they had disappeared, I decided to tidy up inside and was glad to find some candles and one match. Michael had the box of matches with him but I would be able to have just one hot meal. Since I had nothing much to do and was definitely not going anywhere, I watched the comings and goings across the border. It was a busy checkpoint with many cars passing through. The shortest time for a search was forty minutes, but most took over an hour. That day, none of the vehicles was from Britain. As usual, Eastern European vehicles passed through more quickly and in great numbers being searched far less thorough and, occasionally, hardly at all. Only Polish cars had a hard time; many of them were turned away at the border.

Next day Mr McKenzie, from the British Embassy, was allowed to speak to me on the office phone. He told me that Michael and the children were safe and well. Whilst I was in the office, I saw details of a fine which had been imposed on someone else. They had been fined an enormous sum (1003 lei) simply for having small quantities of soap, coffee and chocolate!

I decided it was inhumane to confine me in the van all the time so for my captors' benefit I made a point of making many 'comfort' trips to use the toilet facilities. I also wandered over to the water fountain to drink cold water whenever I felt like it as the high summer temperature had made the water in our tank hot. Two lorries from Liverpool passed through. I think the drivers guessed I was in trouble. One almost came over to speak to me, but he changed his mind when he realized he was being watched. Still, it was good to see a couple of friendly faces again.

Three days passed and I was still in custody. Then on the third evening a man came across the border. The guards allowed him to pass me a note from Michael telling me I could go back to Hungary. So with the necessary items packed, I gladly left my 'prison' to rejoin my family. Michael and the children described how they had been escorted through 'no man's land', right up to the Hungarian border. There they were left, to make their own way back to the village where we had spent the previous night before our adventure. The first thing Michael had to do was to find a telephone - easy to say, but not so easy to find. These were not the days of mobile phones and 'hi-tech' systems. Far from it - in that village, there was only one telephone and anyone wishing to make a call had to book a time and wait their turn. Eventually Michael made contact with the embassy. He informed them of our situation and asked for help in getting money from our building society so that we could pay the fine. He didn't know how long the transaction would take. Obviously, the longer the delay, the longer I would have had to stay imprisoned in the caravanette, without light, heat or food.

Before we set off from Baildon, all those days before, I had gone into the National Provincial Building Society to have our passbook updated. They were too busy to deal with it, so I asked them to hold on to it until we returned; consequently, when they received the telephone call from the British embassy in Budapest the building society actually had our book in their possession, which meant that there was no problem about sending us the money by teletext. On the Monday Michael went to Budapest by train and collected the money. That evening we went to the border to pay the fine and retrieve our caravanette. When we got there we were told that the exchange rate had gone up on the Sunday and consequently we had to pay an extra one thousand pounds! That was bad enough but there was a further problem. The amount we had asked to be forwarded to us from our account was 'clean money', i.e. all the notes were perfect - none was dog-eared, written on or stained - if they were not 'clean' the officials would have refused them. Now we had to pay an extra sum and needed to have enough 'clean' notes from the money we had set out with! In the end the fine totalled about £3,500. (In the eighties this was quite a large sum for us.) We paid up and left.

In view of what had happened at the frontier it is most likely that if we had travelled on into Romania, we would have been followed and our mere presence would have endangered the Christians we met. But why had Eva caused so much trouble at the border? We think it was because Genovieva's brother had been imprisoned. The secret police had ransacked his home, also those of his mother and brother. The police had been looking for addresses and had possibly found ours. That it had taken so long to sort things out was partly due to the weather and the uncertain electricity supply, but also because going through so much information takes a tremendously long time with Communist bureaucracy.

Eventually, after travelling back across Europe, we arrived in England, tired but safe, and all together. Michael was invited to speak to various groups and churches about our experiences. In passing and as part of the story, he mentioned that we had to pay a fine but no one, not even the children, knew how much we had paid. Then something strange began to happen in our home. The letter-box would click and there, lying on the mat, would be some money. Not just once but several times. We never saw who did it. Also, sums of money would arrive through the post to us anonymously. When it was all added up, and in a very short time, the amount of the fine had come in almost to the last penny. To this day, we do not know who gave us the money. We are so thankful to them and to the 'God who provides'.

Political turmoil

Suddenly change was in the air. Prayers had been answered. New freedoms were on the horizon. President Ceausescu, the cruel Romanian dictator, was dead, also his wife. All over Eastern Europe, Communism began to crumble. The repercussions reverberated throughout the former Communist bloc. Suddenly there was great media interest in these countries that had previously been little regarded.

As for Czechoslovakia, no shots were fired when it discarded its robe of Communism in November 1989. Vaclav Havel, playwright, poet and political dissident, became President and later the country split into two separate republics. It had been a 'velvet' revolution. Many fine buildings, castles and chateaux have survived, unlike some of its neighbours which history has not treated so kindly. Prague is one of the most beautiful cities in Europe but the people can also boast of fine mountains, hills and forests and, of course, the Danube. The summers are hot, but winters are bitterly cold. We could only imagine how the poor struggled during those long months. How vital were the gifts which we took year by year from the people of Yorkshire.

The materialistic ways of the West seeped into these nations starved of consumer goods. Both the best and worst of the Western economies now plied their trade with their poorer neighbours. Expectations were high and new-found freedoms were exhilarating but for some, the reality was not always better. The necessary changes would take a very long time. Under Communism everyone had a job, but now there was high unemployment. Wages had been only a pittance but even that was better than nothing. There were supermarkets but often the shopping trolley would contain only one item, and that small and inexpensive. Not everyone coped well with the changes. People got impatient waiting for things to happen. Among the unwanted imports were drugs and new religious cults, both supplied by those who did not have the people's best interests at heart. Some people turned to crime.

It was going to be interesting to see how our work would alter in the light of these new developments. We never realized how our travelling ministry would dramatically come to a halt.

8

The family came too

Children's children are a crown to the aged, and parents are the pride of their children. (Proverbs 17:6)

[Some of our ability to cross borders and checkpoints with comparative ease was no doubt down to the fact that we looked like an ordinary family on a touring holiday - which in a sense we were, although hardly 'ordinary'. As neither Michael nor I had parents still alive or relatives living nearby to take care of the children, we felt it best if the three of them stayed with us. Although there were risks about health and safety, nevertheless, it was good to be together as a family. In this chapter Tamar recounts some of the joys and frustrations experienced on our trips.]

'My first memory of Eastern Europe is from 1980, when I was 3½ years old. I clearly remember being on the Polish/Russian border, and the guards taking our camper van underground so they could search it. For a while we were allowed to wait in a building but then, as night came, we had to go back outside. Dad had been taken off to be searched, Andrew, who was eighteen months old, was asleep on the carry-cot, and Rebecca and I were told to try and get some sleep on the hard stone of the searching benches. I can picture it all clearly in my mind, though I cannot recall how it ended. But I do know that we were able to enter Russia, as it was the year of the Olympics and I remember seeing flags with rings and a bear everywhere.

'Borders have a significant role in my memories. There was 1983 when we crammed in bin bag after bin bag of clothing, and every other item under the sun, from a family in Hampshire to be delivered to a family member in Romania. When we arrived at the Hungarian/Romanian border however, we were turned away. I remember Mum and Dad's frustration and sadness, but at the same time, their ultimate priority was to distribute the aid we had to other needy people, and work out how to deliver the items from the English people to their family. Mum showed much the same attitude in 1997, when one of her major concerns, from her hospital bed, was how to distribute the aid in the caravanette, and how to ensure some doctors in Romania got the things sent for them from my former head of sixth form.

'Before every border crossing, we would stop and pray. Sometimes it would be the old "Open Doors" prayer: "Lord, as you made blind eyes see, please now make seeing eyes blind." Every time we asked that the Lord's will be done and for the protection of the family. I never had any doubt that God would hear and answer those prayers. From an early age I had been taught that things happened because God allowed them to and Dad was forever quoting Isaiah: "God's ways are not our ways, God's ways are far higher."

'So as we approached a border I would experience a knot of apprehension, mingled with exhilaration. The concrete forecourts, dull buildings, glass windows and armed soldiers, posed a threat and presented a challenge. As we waited in the long queues we would play guessing games, trying to work out where a car was from (once we met someone else from Bradford), which guard was the worst (nine times out of ten it would be a woman!) and why a particular car would be in trouble.

'One such "game" acted as a prelude for probably the most eventful border crossing in my trips abroad, Hungary/Romania 1985. Although Mum has described it from her point of view, this is how I saw it through the eyes of an eight-year-old. We arrived at the border mid-afternoon, but it was several hours later, as dusk set in, that a guard finally greeted us. One of the first questions fired at Dad was, 'Have you any Bibles?' We were all in the back of the vehicle and Mum indicated for us to be quiet. Dad answered 'yes' and asked us to collect our Bibles to show the guards. This was not enough to deter them and soon a thorough search had begun. In the meantime we were encouraged to read or play games. I rather think Mum even made us something to eat but I do remember how. At one stage we went to the toilets and Mum shredded all the addresses we had. Rebecca and I then had to go to the toilets and flush and flush till every scrap of paper had gone. Rebecca also had to hide money in her underwear but, much to my disappointment, I was deemed not old enough! I was too excited to be scared and too naïve to recognize the severity of the events. That night we had to get changed in the dark as Dad had tripped the electricity during the search. Mum and Dad talked in hushed tones about what to do, for we had been given an ultimatum: we must pay a fine or surrender the van. I was not concerned; I knew my parents would sort it out, and after all - we had prayed. About eight o'clock next morning we were woken by a loud bang on the door, indicating that it was time to move. After hurriedly packing a few items, Mum was kept hostage with the camper van while the rest of us were marched about six miles through no man's land, back to the nearest Hungarian town. We were given an armed escort but for me it merely added to the sense of adventure. I felt like I was one of the "Famous Five"! We spent the next three days at a pastor's home, and there, while Dad rushed around making phone calls, trying to organize the transfer of money and Mum's safe release, I began to read my Bible properly on my own for the first time. I read Genesis and Matthew all the way through. I can remember missing Mum and longing to see her again, but at the same time never doubted that I would. Whilst I didn't recognize it at the time, in hindsight I believe the Lord really undertook for us and gave us such a sense of peace and his loving presence - much as he did twelve years later. What I really learned through the event though was that miracles still happen and God is still at work. In the following six months we received so many anonymous gifts and donations that they covered the fine. It struck me, as a young eight-year-old, how God really did provide for and look after his people. I can remember sharing it with friends at school, both then and in later years.

'Borders could be fun too. In 1992, as we were going from Romania into Moldova, a border guard found my Bible. I gazed in horror, Enid Blyton long since forgotten, as he flicked through the pages. He stopped, looked up, cleared his throat, and then in faltering English read out the first verse of Psalm 100. "Shoot . . . for . . . joy", he read. It should have been "shout" - an interesting slip!

'The build-up for our annual trips was itself quite an ordeal. Every holiday we were carted off, as a family, to various places in the British Isles, so Dad could share reports of the work. Dad organized this, as he did the summer expeditions, with very little consultation. Then would come the packing. Since they were full-time teachers and heavily involved in other work, packing was always very last-minute. Mum would produce a list in advance saying what we needed but the collection rarely took place until the week of departure, and packing and loading was left to the Friday we all broke up from school. When we were really young, we three children would stay at other people's homes for the evening to keep us out of the way; then as we got older we were roped into helping. Shopping for food was always the fun bit - racing round, each pushing a trolley. We used to leave late on Saturday and Dad would drive down the A1 to Suffolk where he would be preaching morning and evening, before catching a ferry the next day from Harwich. Mum was often so exhausted she would sleep as we travelled. So I would try to get the privileged front seat in the cab alongside Dad. I loved sitting there, taking in the countryside, navigating and chatting away to my Dad. It was a position I delighted in and hogged for as much of the trip as I could.

'When we set off the caravanette would always be overloaded and bursting at the seams. Dad and Mum just wanted to take as much as they could and struggled knowing when to stop. We each had a tiny drawer to cram our clothes in for the summer. The five of us shared a wardrobe and there were a few cupboards for our own food. Anything else was on our seats, together with blankets and toys to give away. I was so excited when we got a camper van with a toilet and shower! But my excitement was short-lived when I discovered Dad had other ideas - more space for storage! As the trip went on, the camper van would empty and so we were able to spread out a little more. How I longed for those times when I didn't have to share a double bed!

'When I think about the cramped conditions, the length of the trip, the heat of the summer and human nature, it is altogether amazing we didn't kill each other!

We did of course have our rows, but on the whole those five or six weeks were generally the times we got on best as sisters and brother, probably because we had no one else! Each of us had his or her own area of the vehicle, and swaps had to be negotiated. Rebecca, as the eldest and most creative, used to invent games and stories for us, and every summer would make me a paper doll with a whole wardrobe of clothes. Before the trip, each of us would be bought some books, paper and pencils, and sweets. The sweets were very important to us as we knew that we wouldn't be eating properly for weeks and certainly would not be able to buy decent sweets. So within the first day or two each of us would write a list, working out our sweet allocation for every day of the trip, to ensure a balance was kept and that there were some left to the bitter end. There were two problems with this: chocolate does not last well in temperatures of 100 degrees or more; also foreign children often asked for 'bonbons' (sweets) - a request which Mum and Dad made us fulfil. We found a way around this; we off-loaded the most detested sweets of all, the Parma violets!

'For us children, food was a definite downer. How we hated the standard diet of Eastern Europeans - black bread, gherkin, pepper, salami and soup! People gave all that they had, more than they could afford, and yet we were so ungrateful. It must have been a real embarrassment for our parents, as time after time we would refuse to eat. There was one time we had been playing in a farmyard with a duck, which was subsequently served to us in soup - beak included. Another time we fed a young calf, and later saw it looking up at us from a plate. Mum eventually came up with a fantastic idea. just as we approached a friend's home, she would start cooking (usually tinned food that we had taken with us), so when we were invited for a meal, she could honestly say that she had prepared food already. Mum and Dad would then go and eat with the family, whilst the three of us tucked in to 'proper' food! During our trips abroad we did seek out the best ice cream parlours in each country, which helped to keep us going during the weeks of travel. The rest of the time we just had to pray, "Lord, we'll get it down, if you keep it down" - a prayer which was generally answered.

'People really did give us the very best and welcomed us with outstretched arms into their homes. They tended to live in flats or small dark houses. Rooms would be bare, furniture limited, ornaments wooden, rugs threadbare, pictures colourful, bedding lumpy, sofas uncomfortable and curtains invariably drawn. Children were often expected to be seen and not heard, so we would have to just sit for hours - or at least try and sit - I was never very good at it. It was always worse when Dad was speaking French or German and I couldn't understand what was being said. Although I found it long, hot and boring, I much preferred the travelling to the visiting. I used to resent the fact that all my friends were going on package holidays to Spain, France or America, enjoying the beach and then having fun back home, while I had to spend the whole summer with my family. Mind you, it came in handy in the first assembly in September when asked where we went on holiday. I used to take great delight in listing nine or ten different countries.

'Other memories of Eastern Europe would have to include toilets, about which I won't go into detail. The majority were disgusting - whether inside or outside - and I had a habit of locking myself in. Rebecca was once stranded in an outside one during a hurricane, which amused Andrew and me a great deal. Another time I was refused entry to a public toilet because the cleaner thought I was a boy, a common mistake as girls very rarely had short hair. Since I spoke no Czech, the only way I could get the message across was to wear a skirt! What amazed me most about the toilets was not necessarily how unhygienic they were but rather the resourcefulness of the people and their pets . . . But I won't divulge anymore!

'Other brief memories would be of the atrocious roads - often just unmarked, unlit dust-tracks, full of potholes. In some countries there would more cattle and carts than cars on the road such was the petrol shortage and backwardness in development. We frequently got lost (Dad chose the shortest routes whatever the conditions) and frequently broke down, the tyres and radiator being the main sources of problems. Yet help would usually come in one form or another and we would generally arrive at our destination - by the grace of God. This is especially amazing when you consider Dad's maps were generally tatty and addresses were scrawled on scraps of paper.

'People would often try and show us cultural places. These included zoos (which in the UK would have been closed for animal cruelty), museums, Orthodox churches - and the forests, which were the only ones I really enjoyed, especially in Czechoslovakia. We would stay in a family farmhouse, have the opportunity to go mushrooming and bilberry picking, and join in their family prayers. I still have vivid memories of the rattling of the trams, the greyness of the buildings, the love for Coca-Cola and the poverty shared by many; also of the time I received my GCSE results in a church in Poland. It was frustrating having to share them with people who called me "Tamara" (as the majority did, much to my annoyance), rather than with my friends. I also remember having to sit through long church services, and of how

Andrew was upset by having to sit with Dad and the other men on one side, whilst Rebecca and I were able to sit with Mum. Eastern Europe was when I began to appreciate my Dad's preaching - as it was the only point of the service I would ever understand. The sermon he preached most fluently in French and German was on the story in Acts 8 about Philip and the Ethiopian.

'During the years of Communism, every visit had to be carefully considered. We were often not allowed to speak in the streets as we made our ways to homes, lest people realize Westerners were visiting. In some homes we would have to speak in hushed tones. Once on a campsite, the night watch was so close that mum was quizzed about why she had come across (with insect repellent) to the tent Rebecca and I shared. Every move was scrutinized, so great care was needed. That did not stop us however from frequently spending the night pulled up on the side of the road. Once I was awoken by Mum climbing out of the van in her nightie armed with two table legs. It turned out that someone had been trying to break in, but Dad was more interested in BBC World Service cricket and so let her deal with it.

'Another incident when Dad let Mum take control occurred in Kosovo when I was six years old. We were coming down from the mountains when our brakes failed and cars started flashing us. It turned out the undercarriage was on fire, so Dad got us children out, whilst Mum was left to deal with the fire. While we were waiting for the vehicle to be fixed a man came out from a nearby house and let us children go and watch TV. He gave Andrew a pocket watch as we left, which I promptly hid. I got my come-uppance later that evening when I was playing with it. I got the ring stuck and had to be taken all round the camp to try to find someone who could manage to pull it off. It was at the same camp site that Dad washed the van and in the process managed to literally flood the engine - not the best of stays!

'Dad loved to swim - and swim he did - wherever. This meant that every summer we would spend a day in Frankfurt at some friends' house and visit the local outdoor pools. It also resulted in our swimming one day on a Polish beach; it was only when we came out that we discovered why we had been the only ones there. The beach was contaminated. Fortunately it didn't do us too much harm!!

'My attitude to Eastern Europe really changed with the collapse of Communism. Up to that point, as I have already said, I resented the fact I was away so much, and found the majority of each summer a very testing time. However the Romanian revolution was on my thirteenth birthday, shortly after I had made a recommitment to the Lord. It really began to hit me then how privileged I was to be part of this work, helping people, meeting with fellow believers and experiencing other cultures. 1990 was my first trip to Romania in nine years. Up to that point it had just been a forbidden land that we had often gazed at across the Danube. I soon fell in love with the place and the people; there is such poverty and yet such warmth. As I walked around the orphanages, I was swamped by children who had never seen Westerners before. When I saw the splendour of Ceausescu's palace and the destruction of the revolution, I came to appreciate the significance of what my parents had been doing. The love they had for the Lord was a love I now shared. Similar lessons were learned and challenges set when, in 1993, we went to Croatia. We came face to face with the UN and war victims, were surrounded by rubble, and could hear the gunshots ringing in the distance. It was a costly reminder of the futility of life and the need for the gospel. My mindset has been greatly influenced by my trips abroad and I have learned so many valuable lessons that in hindsight I can honestly say the pros far outweigh the cons. The cons were based upon trivial issues - the pros on spiritual.

My greatest joy from Eastern Europe was seeing Andrew become a Christian in 1992. It happened after we had visited an amazing family in a tiny Romanian village. They were extremely poor but they really did have radiant faces. Andrew was struck by how little they had materially, and yet how much they had spiritually and this made him reflect on his own standing with God and caused him to call out for salvation. My greatest sorrow was obviously the loss of my father; yet even that has been used to glorify God. I'll never forget how instantly my hatred and anger washed away as I prayed on the hospital balcony in Hungary, just after hearing Mum say that she had forgiven the lads. What peace the Lord has provided, how wonderfully he undertook!

'Dad was the steady rock of the family, very stable, and the driving force. This didn't mean he was unfeeling; he used to cry every time he dropped me off at university and dreaded the journey home alone. Mum provided the crucial support and organization. Whilst Dad was quiet and calm, Mum was more lively and talkative, with a real sense of humour. Despite this she was very shy and was often in the shadow of my Dad. Mum is so very generous and humble, frequently putting others first. When I went to Bradford Girls' Grammar School, she went without new clothes and shoes for five years so she could pay my fees. She is gifted musically, picks up new languages easily, and is "arty" - she's written many poems. Obviously the depression Mum has suffered from over the years has affected her character, nevertheless God has used many of these changes to his glory.

'Something unusual happened before Dad died. I was doing a long stint working as a volunteer with United Beach Missions, but after three weeks, my parents insisted that I should come home to see them on the Saturday afternoon and go on the next morning. This was an unusual request, as I "never" broke my missions. When the summer plans were originally made nothing had been mentioned about my coming home. So the last time I saw my Dad was just ten days before he was killed. How pleased I am that I did make that journey home though - it meant I had one last opportunity to say goodbye.

9

The final journey

Not till the loom is silent and the shuttles cease to fly
Will God unroll the canvas and explain the reason why.
The dark threads are as needful in the skilful weaver's hand
As the threads of gold and silver in the pattern he has planned.

In all our years of marriage, one thing I never shared with Michael was his meticulous method of documenting the mundane and the miraculous events of life. Perhaps as a mother of three children, owner of beloved cats and various other animal species, there was not much time spare for scribbling. It was rather surprising then to realize that on our fateful last trip I had actually made some notes on some torn-off pieces of paper, written at various stages in different inks. Since my memory is now not so good as it used to be, I have found it helpful to read over again what I wrote about the events as I experienced them.

Our journey did not start well. Before what turned out to be our final trip together, Michael and I had actually thought about calling it a day, as far as our visits to Eastern Europe were concerned. It was not because I was afraid to return to Romania, despite being held hostage there. But there were a number of changes. We were not as young as we used to be. Bones now creaked a bit - so did our vehicle! Michael had retired from teaching, although he still visited numerous schools in our area to take assemblies. He had also started to suffer a little with angina and I had developed diabetes. The children had grown up; Andrew, the youngest, was about to leave for university. For twenty-seven years, we had spent our holidays on camper trips each summer - perhaps this should be our last?

Every year Michael would volunteer to be a helper with United Beach Missions. Normally he did this after we returned from Eastern Europe, while I would stay at home to empty the van and clean it up after five weeks of travelling, often on very dusty tracks and roads. But in 1997, unusually, Michael went before we left. On the application form he sent to the UBM office he wrote: 'Christ has given me assurance my sins are forgiven, and peace, and I know where I am going when I die.'

Andrew thought about coming once more but in the end stayed at home. He and his friend, Richard, helped to load the van. The two lads packed the large bed above the cab with toiletries and baby items. Anybody passing by would have wondered why they should need such large amounts of nappies, feeding bottles and baby foods. Inside, we crammed in as many clothes as we could. Some beautiful knitted garments had been donated for us to give to families who had very little. We always took milk powder, drinks and food for babies whose mothers were unable to feed them. The cupboards above the seat held screw-in light bulbs, which had formerly been as scarce as hens' teeth! Medical items were packed in the box at the rear of the van. Although some of the products were available in Eastern Europe, not only were they often sold at greatly inflated prices but they were sometimes counterfeits, which might prove dangerous. The box under the back bed was packed with Bibles, Bible-reading notes, Christian books for all ages and teaching aids. Because so many people abroad can or want to speak English, we had a quantity of suitable material in English as well. By this time, the van was already pretty full.

Next to go in was our food. We had to take sufficient so that if we broke down in an isolated area or had visitors needing a good square meal, we were prepared. Cooking and eating implements were stuffed in somewhere. The water tank had to be filled and the gas bottle checked to see that it was full. The bathroom was so full of things that had nowhere else to go, it was virtually impossible to get in there anyway! They included the usual things you would expect to find in a bathroom, as well as some you definitely would not! The former head of the sixth form at Bingley Grammar School, Eileen Hilton, had worked very hard to raise funds to pay for some text books for teaching English as a foreign language. We had volunteered to take them to the Romanian hospital to which they had been assigned. We hid them in the storage box which normally contained towels, packets of soap and toilet rolls. (The books were gratefully received, having survived the whole journey, as did the big birthday cake, which we placed in the oven.)

Once the inside was packed as full as possible, we started on the outside; whatever else we had to take went on the roof-rack where a tarpaulin helped to keep the contents dry and clean. Our preparations had included writing down the estimated times of border crossings so that Christian friends could support us by praying. As usual, we finally committed the van, the trip and our family and friends into God's hands, asking for his guidance, trusting him for whatever lay ahead. Then on July 27 1997 Michael and I drove off with a rev of the engine and a burst of exhaust fumes, to what was to be our last venture together in our beloved camper van.

Before leaving Britain, we called in to see friends at Brotherton, who shared their delicious Sunday lunch with us. They also generously gave us more goods for Eastern Europe! Somehow we managed to fit everything in, but you could almost hear the van groan! As we neared the ferry port of Hull, disaster struck. One of the rear tyres had a puncture - it was a complete write-off. Michael went to a neighbouring house to advise the ferry company that we would be arriving late and asked if they would wait for us. The person on the other end of the phone wasn't very optimistic but Michael was and a kind man left off digging his garden to come to our aid and helped fit the spare tyre. Off we sped to the terminal, relieved to find that vehicles were still being loaded. After having rushed so much, we felt it was ironic that the ferry had to wait because the tide was too low. Thankfully, the overnight journey to Rotterdam was uneventful.

Once when we broke down in Holland a family had helped us; they had become our friends and we visited them each time we were in the area. Now we needed their help again: we had to get a new tyre. But as we approached the house, everything seemed suspiciously quiet. Perhaps they were on holiday? Just as we were about to drive away, the family swooped along on their bicycles. They had moved to a smaller home and, 'just happened' to come back to collect some of their things. The timing was brilliant; a difference of five minutes either way and we would have missed each other. A nearby garage supplied the tyre, and off we headed for Germany.

After visiting friends on the Eastern side, we made our way to our next destinations, the Czech Republic and Slovakia. In one town we visited two girls who had been au pairs in Leeds and had spent Boxing Day with us two years previously. They invited us to a Catholic youth group, where I sang and Michael described how it was that he had become a Christian all those years ago. The young people asked questions, and Michael was able to tell them more about Jesus and his love for them. At the end he really emphasized that he knew he would go to heaven straight away when he died. Little did we know that Michael had only three more days to live.

10

Night attack

'Do not fear the things which you are about to suffer...
Be faithful unto death and I will give you a crown of life.
(Revelation 2:10 - part of the August 3 reading from Michael's *Daily Light*)

The day had begun in such a promising way. We were excited about visiting 'the rainbow man' (see page 36). We were looking forward to seeing this lovely family, spending time with them and giving gifts. We had almost reached the house when we saw the wife and youngest child carrying milk. They waved, so we parked the vehicle and followed them. As we went in we noticed a gate that had been chained up, but we couldn't understand why. We were invited in and made very welcome, as was the usual Eastern custom. There was no sign of the 'rainbow man'. 'How is your husband?' Michael asked.

'Gone', the wife replied.

Michael and I both looked at each other. Had he gone off with another woman? Surely not. We could not imagine that he would leave his wife and four lovely children. There must be some other explanation. Maria disappeared, but shortly returned, bringing a photo of our 'rainbow man' lying in a coffin. He had suffered a fatal stroke eighteen months ago. He was forty-five years old and left a wife and four children, the youngest only three years old. We made sure to leave plenty of food items to help them through the winter months. Unbeknown to us, Maria's father had had a heart attack. He and his wife had been to the hospital but returned especially to see us, as they knew we were coming. We enjoyed our special time with them but then had to leave as I needed to collect my next visa from the border. Because I had a New Zealand passport, some countries required me to obtain a visa, unlike Michael who was British.

After the inevitable delays, we crossed into Hungary. The mountains were so beautiful. As we passed through the gorgeous scenery, we noticed storks in the fields, sitting on their nests. We had hoped to make it to the home of some friends, where we could park the van outside for the night, but this was not to be. It was getting late. The road was a bit rough and as we hit a bump, the jolt fused our indicator lights. We didn't want to be in trouble with the police, so we decided to stop in a lay-by.

As darkness fell, we prepared the beds, changed into our night clothes and settled down for the night. It seemed only a short time had passed before we were rudely awakened by a banging on the camper van. We both moved to the door, which was locked, and peered into the darkness. A young man dressed in black called out, 'Police!' He carried an identification card with a photograph. He went on speaking in what I recognized as Hungarian (I know a little of various languages, just to get us by in most situations) and seemed to be warning us that what we were doing was forbidden. 'Problem, problem!' I called back to him. But he was having none of it. He shrugged his shoulders but I knew he understood. Then I noticed another man lurking in the darkness by their little car. In those split seconds my mind began wondering whether these might be men from the Mafia, which had been spreading its tentacles throughout many countries. In a shop window in Slovakia we had seen one of their signs, indicating that it was under Mafia protection. I couldn't really see much of this second man but my instincts told me that the first man was too young to be a policeman.

Then he shouted, '*Tilos* (forbidden)!'

'I do not speak Hungarian, I speak English!' I replied.

Although he seemed unable to speak English, he indicated that we had parked illegally and then gave us two pieces of paper, one bearing a number. We gathered these were receipts of some kind. On one he had written the registration number of our van. I was increasingly suspicious. Then he demanded a fine of 2,000 forints each. While I was putting everything away safely in our knife drawer I called to Michael, 'Quick, see if you can get the car registration number.' But the two men had disappeared into the darkness without putting their lights on. We couldn't see the number.

However, such an incident was not unusual and we did not initially feel intimidated. Over the course of the many thousands of miles we had travelled, police or soldiers frequently stopped us. Besides, Communism was now a thing of the past and everywhere was much safer - or so we thought. To-morrow, we decided, we would go to the police; but first we moved the van further round the lay-by. Wearily we turned back our bed covers and settled down for a second time.

The second knocking came about an hour later. This time it woke me only but I quickly reached over to Michael and raised the alarm. 'Oh, that's it, let's go,' he decided crossly, getting out of bed. Levering himself over the seat, he slumped down behind the steering wheel. As he was putting the key into the ignition to turn the engine over, I was making my way to the front to join him. Then suddenly a masked man wearing black smashed through the driver's window. As pieces of the shattered glass flew, he hit Michael with an iron bar and continued to punch Michael as hard as he could with his fists. I was so shocked that I watched helplessly. I could hardly believe what was happening in front of my eyes. Never in twenty-seven years of travelling had I seen violence such as this. I 'froze' like a statue.

The masked man kept hitting, hitting and hitting poor Michael, who was trying desperately to push the man's hands away. Somehow Michael managed to get one hand on to the horn, hooting like mad in the vain hope that a passer-by would hear. The sound brought me to my senses and I started shouting 'Help, help!' as loud as I could. With that the masked man disappeared from the broken window and vanished into the darkness.

'Oh, there's a lot of blood', Michael called out weakly, as I leaned over to help him. (It's extraordinary what goes through your mind at times like this. Michael never did like blood. His mother had wanted him to be a doctor but if any our children cut themselves, Michael disappeared.) I reached for a cloth to wipe the blood from his face and hands but as I did so, I realized something was seriously wrong. He wasn't responding. 'Oh no!' I thought. 'Is there something wrong with his heart? Only a week or two before we set off, Michael had gone to our local hospital for an angiogram. They told him that probably he had suffered a mild heart attack in the past, as there was some scar tissue.

Although I'm no nurse I thought, 'I must give him mouth-to-mouth resuscitation.' That was pretty horrible. Blood had gone down the back of his throat and it felt as though his whole stomach must be filled with blood. And Michael did not respond. The truth dawned on me. Michael was dead.

11

Left for dead

Michael had been murdered before my eyes by an unknown attacker, who had vanished. Would the murderer return?

I felt he would. But there in the cold reality of that early morning in Hungary, as I cradled the body of my dead husband, God gave me a gift - the gift of his peace. I couldn't see God. I couldn't hear God, but I knew he was there.

In the panic of the attack it never occurred to me to drive away. In any case, I had never driven the vehicle in my life. And where could I have gone? Would the attackers have chased me? I decided to stay where I was. With the utmost care, I tried to move Michael's body into the living area of the camper van, but couldn't get him very far. He was too heavy.

Quickly I changed into my day clothes. My distrust of men, caused by my rape attack when I was nine, made me fear the murderers would be back. Looking round, I gathered together all the valuables - my watch and rings, our personal money, passports and the money we had brought to give away. I hid them in what I hoped was a safe place and then looked for something with which to protect myself. There were two metal cylinders, which converted into table supports, and I grabbed them so that I could hit the men if they returned. Then

I thought again., 'No, better not do that or the men will probably kill me.' As I frantically looked round the vehicle, my eyes fell on a can of fly spray. It was so pungent that we always told the kids to close their eyes when-ever we squirted the stuff to rid our van of mosquitoes. I put the can near the door so that I could spray the man. I believe it was the Lord who gave me this idea. Then for some time, I sat on the bed turning over the pages of my Bible. I found much comfort in reading some of the Psalms.

Again there was knocking at the door. A different voice shouted, 'Police! Do you need help? Do you have a problem?' I didn't really think it was the police, but I did need help. 'If you really are the police,' I implored, 'then you can help me. My husband is dead and I am very frightened.' As I opened the door to the living area, a man in black confronted me, spraying a narcotic in my face. Being prepared, I grabbed the fly spray and retaliated. (My own eyes were affected, and I was unable to see for several days.) I had also thought carefully while hiding our valuables. Although I had hidden almost all of them, I had left fifty pounds in English currency in my handbag, which was hanging in the wardrobe. My thinking was that if the men did come back, they would find the money, presuming it was all I had - then probably leave me alone.

I remember sitting back on my bed again, having locked the door and going back to reading the Psalms. Apparently the man did return. He savagely kicked me in the head, broke both my nose and jaw in two places and left me with finger marks around my neck. At some stage I was knocked out. Drifting in and out of consciousness, I was in effect unaware of anything for some hours.

I had been left for dead.

Dawn was breaking as I regained consciousness. My eyes were so stuck up that I had to prise them apart to see if it was morning. Mercifully it was, so I knew it was safe to go for help. How I reached the road, I don't know. It was more by hearing than by sight. I tried to find a place where I could hear the traffic. Two vehicles came along. First there was a car. It stopped but then drove off. The driver did not alert anyone. The second vehicle was a bread van. The driver must have had a nasty shock seeing me staggering along; my face was a dreadful mess. 'I need help, please call the police - my husband is dead!'

The next thing I knew was that I was in hospital. They thought I might die.

12

The hospital bed and the Press

Mercifully I had felt no pain, possibly (I then thought) because of the narcotic spray which my attackers squirted in my face. I remember pulling my eyes apart and calling to passing vehicles on the road but that's all. The next thing I knew was that I was lying beneath cool, white sheets in the safety of the local hospital at Nyiregyhaza. I was in the intensive care ward and the whole ghastly tragedy was about to unfold as doctors and police attempted to trace my family.

Andrew, the youngest, was by himself at home in Baildon. The phone rang. It was someone from a daily newspaper. 'Is that the home of Michael Trevor Pollard and Jo Pollard?'

'Yes, it is' Andrew answered. Just as the man on the other end of the phone was about to say something else, there was a knock at the door. 'Excuse me,' said Andrew to the caller, ' there's a policeman at the door.' When Andrew picked up the phone again, the line had gone dead.

Fortunately, the police had pre-empted what might have been a very distressing and awkward situation for both Andrew and the newspaper reporter. The police gently explained about Michael's death. One of the policemen, who was a Christian, prayed with Andrew, who then contacted his sister Rebecca at work and gave her the devastating news.

Tamar was in Kent helping with the United Beach Missions outreach at Broadstairs. A friend's brother had heard the news on Sky Television. He quickly contacted the general secretary of UBM, who in turn phoned the Home Office in London for confirmation. The officials wanted to know how the news had leaked out. Apparently, Hungary and England had agreed to release the news at the same time but the Sky report had gone out earlier. The Kent police visited the UBM headquarters in Broadstairs and told Tamar that I was badly injured in hospital. Tamar immediately presumed that since Michael had not been mentioned, her Dad must be dead. Friends and officials hastily arranged to fly the children to my bedside.

Meanwhile, back in Hungary, I was - thankfully - being well cared for by the doctors and nurses. For the second time in my life, someone had attacked my body. The initial reasons for my freedom from pain were wearing off but I was not allowed painkillers because the police wanted me to hang on to my thread of memory of what happened. Mostly I was drowsy. My jaw, which had been broken, was operated on, repaired and screwed. My nose had been packed with gauze - the worst part during that time was the agony of having the packing removed.

I don't remember having my photo taken while I was in hospital. The first time I looked in the mirror I myself was shocked at the terrible state of my face. I can only imagine what friends back home thought as they opened their newspapers and turned on the television to see my swollen, bruised head, looking as though I'd just done a few rounds with Mike Tyson! My memory of much of what happened in hospital is a blur, though I can remember a microphone being stuck in front of my face and being asked to say a few words: *'I have been told that my attackers have been caught. Three of them, one aged 18 and two 22-year-olds. I don't know what their sentence will be. I don't feel any malice towards them because I'm a Christian and as such I just hope they realize that what they have done is wrong and against God's will and in time that they will be born again - become Christians themselves.'*

In no time my words and news of the attack were flashed round the world. Christians of all ages, nationalities and denominations prayed both for the family and for our attackers, as yet unknown. After a day or two I was moved from intensive care and put into another room which had a door leading to a balcony. Patients from the next ward in various conditions would wander through to stand just looking at me sorrowfully. Sometimes they would kindly bring me flowers or fruit drinks. Representatives from a number of religious denominations visited me although I didn't particularly know what was going on around me. To my amazement, one day I had visitors from Derby, England. A family had heard that someone from England had been murdered so they decided to visit the survivor. The husband was Hungarian but the wife was English. Several times they came to visit and talk with me, which I greatly appreciated.

The night before we were due to return England, Tamar contacted a missionary from the European Christian Mission in Vienna for help. The police had finished fingerprinting, removing evidence and generally 'frisking' our vehicle, but it was still our responsibility. Despite its appearance it still contained food, clothes and aid for people of Eastern Europe. Stuart Rowell and Hungarian Christians from the Calvary Chapels kindly arranged for the goods to be distributed to people in need. Tamar and I didn't really know what to do with the van as I would never be able to drive it. We took advice and decided that the best place for it was the scrap-yard. I was glad not to have a constant reminder of that August day.

Some remarkable things happened while I was in the intensive care unit. There were two other ladies with me but surprisingly they were walking about. (I always thought that if you were a patient in the ITC you had to stay put in bed.) These kind souls would tenderly care for me by dipping camomile tea in gauze and placing it over my eyes to soothe them. Whenever I needed something they seemed to know and were there for me. The strange thing is I never saw them again. I enquired, but they were not patients or nurses. No one knew them. Who were they? Angels? We will never know. Whoever they were, I just thank the Lord that they came and looked after me so well.

Another remarkable coincidence - but God's way of looking after me - was that one of the doctors who tended me was also a Christian. Although I don't remember our conversation when we met, we both somehow knew by God's Holy Spirit in us that we both belonged to him. This doctor was Hungarian by birth but brought up in Canada, therefore he could speak English. He was a great help to me and the family. Initially he was called to interview me because the lady who worked for the police took one look at me, couldn't bear what she saw, and promptly fainted! The doctor went so far as to allow my children, who had travelled to be with me, to stay at his home. They took it in turns to stay the night at my bedside.

I was in hospital for nine days before the hospital was willing to release me. Arrangements had been made for me to travel back by air from Budapest to Leeds via London/Heathrow, so, expressing my gratitude to everybody at the hospital, including all those involved in my rescue, I left Hungary. I had one deep regret: I had to leave Michael's body behind. Setting up a murder enquiry, with all the associated bureaucracy, meant that that arrangements for transferring the body to England would take some while. I knew it was only a body for I remembered St Paul's comforting words - 'absent from the body, present with the Lord'. For a Christian, death has lost its awful 'sting'.

But though we could all rejoice that Michael was in heaven, nevertheless we suffered tremendous loss, as those who have been bereaved will recognize. The removal and burial of Michael's body, an important part of the necessary grieving process, would have to be delayed. The fact that there was a criminal investigation by the police also inevitably caused us anguish. I sorely missed Michael but I also grieved for our three attackers. Who were they? Where were they now?

Happily our departure from Hungary was less eventful than our arrival. Although my facial aches compounded the usual discomforts of air travel they were bearable - I was on my way back home at last. But at Heathrow we encountered a problem - our passports. The officials told Rebecca and me that we were illegal immigrants! You can imagine how welcome we didn't feel. Although my paternal grandfather was Scottish, I had never taken up my right to a British passport. All three children have New Zealand citizenship, but only Tamar and Andrew have dual passports. I presume that there had been a change in regulations as in all my years of travelling in and out of Britain, not once had I been stopped. A disagreeable official told me that I needed to have a 'special right of abode'. He was not at all impressed by my protestations that my husband had been murdered and I had left hospital only a few hours before. Nothing could deter him. But eventually 'officialdom' relented and we boarded the next aircraft.

A press conference had been arranged at Leeds/Bradford airport. A smart, practical conference room had been made available for us and although we were tired out we answered the journalists' questions as best we could. I had been assured that the police would be on hand to assist us through the airport and the press conference and to make sure that the privacy of our arrival in Baildon was protected. So we were shielded from the ordeal of a long interrogation and awkward questions. The police inspector was a Christian, whose two daughters had been taught by Michael. He was to be of great help to us again when Michael's body was eventually returned. Finally, the police told the crowd that had gathered that the family would appreciate being left alone the following day. This brought the interview to an end. I must admit that on the whole the media have been absolutely superb. The attitude of the British press was commendable.

The final leg of the journey home was by car. It was marvellous to find a few friends waiting for us in the house. The kettle was on. The cats strolled in, stretching and yawning before welcoming me back with their contented purring. There were hot drinks. I was home.

The following day was quiet. We were so thankful for that day when we could just be ourselves. The everyday routines - washing, dressing, eating, feeding the animals - had a mildly therapeutic effect. They gave us something to do as we collected our thoughts and prayed to the 'God of all comfort'. From then on, the phone rang constantly and we averaged about twenty-five visitors a day. Lots of cards began to arrive. Our poor postman had to bear his heavy load day after day up our sloping garden. One day, as I opened the door, I said, 'I do feel sorry that you are having to carry all those cards.'

'It's a real pleasure,' he replied and obviously meant it.

Some people were tearful; some were embarrassed and found it hard to speak; some were in control, some very emotional; some needed time before they could visit. We appreciated every card, word, tear and phone call, visit, gift and prayer. In grief we need each other. God was able to help me to help others in coming to terms with our own experiences of bereavement.

I don't think people were sure what to expect when I arrived home. Some people found it helpful that I didn't fall apart straight away. I said, 'Look, I'm still me. I'm OK. Just be normal with me!' I suppose the fact that I could talk to people without floods of tears made it easier for them. I couldn't put on an act and say that I was grieving in the way one is 'supposed to'. When my mother died it was months before the inevitable tears and overwhelming sense of loss and grief flooded my being. Then the release brought healing. Now my doctor felt my body would probably take a similar time to come to terms with what had happened.

Headlines began to appear in the newspapers:

'Preacher clubbed to death'

'Fatal attack by bandit trio'

'Pastor's wife bears no grudge'.

I gave numerous interviews as journalists focused on the fact that I had said I had forgiven my attackers. I told them, 'I don't know why they did this to us, just for money or something like that - I'm sorry I have no husband now, only my three children. They have just arrived and we will have to live without Michael. I know he is in heaven and he will be OK there and I will have to trust in God's grace every day to be able to continue living without him. So ask people that know us to pray for us. We need prayer so much at this time.' But I had no hate in my heart. I bore no grudge. With God's help and because I was trusting in Christ, I harboured no bitterness. Instead the peace of God was allowed to have free course in my life. This freed me up to cope with the trial, face my assailants and begin my new life as a widow.

A few days later we received a stark reminder that death enters every home regardless of status. The little-known teacher from Baildon found herself sharing front page headlines with Diana, Princess of Wales.

13

Journalists

Serious, careful, honest, journalism is essential, not because it is a guiding light, but because it is a form of honourable behaviour, involving the reporter and the reader.

(Martha Gellhorn)[6]

My first encounter with the 'infamous' world press was shortly after my arrival in hospital. Frankly, I was not aware of much going on around me. When a microphone was stuck in front of my mouth, I somehow found words to say to express my feelings about the men who had perpetrated the crime.

The Calendar team from Yorkshire Television had telephoned the hospital to discover my condition. It wasn't intended to be a personal interview. The producer simply hoped that I was going to live, so that he could relay good news. At home, friends, family and neighbours were reassured to hear my voice. But my comment that I bore no malice toward our attackers seemed to come as a shock to many people. It caught the attention of journalists and made headlines around the world. The reaction of the press came as a complete surprise to me. I was simply stating what I believed as a Christian. The three men had done wrong. It was right that the State should punish them, but to have bitterness in my heart was not an option for me as a Christian. Though I was hurting terribly in so many ways, God had given me the strength and ability to forgive the men and to show love to them even though they didn't deserve it. Christ himself had prayed concerning those who were crucifying him, 'Father, forgive them for they know not what they do.'

I never sought publicity but was happy to co-operate, as news has to be reported. As long as questions were honestly asked, I would give my answers and opinions. If the articles and interviews have helped people consider the way of forgiveness, as demonstrated by Jesus Christ, then it will have been worth it.

Not long after Michael's death I came across an interesting piece in our local paper, the *Aire Valley Target*. Roger Owen referred to a book entitled *The Lost Art of Forgiveness*. The book, he said, points out that although attributing blame and seeking revenge are a natural response when we are hurt, these are negative ways to expend energy. It's better to act positively, seeking release, reconciliation and recovery. Although forgiving requires strength and courage, it not only follows Christ's teaching but is also enlightened self-interest. 'Failure to forgive is a significant cause of disease and dysfunction. Whilst desire for retribution poisons the "hurt" person with bitterness, forgiveness helps to heal deep hurts.'

Kathy Tedd of Jubilee Outreach Yorkshire and others set up a fund to meet the many expenses we had to bear, including bringing Michael's body home. By October 1997 about £16,000 had been received. Half of this was spent on funeral expenses, air flights etc. Shipley market traders raised more than £100 in two days. Eventually, the fund totalled £25,000. Besides family expenses, gifts were made, as a 'living' tribute, to Christian workers in Hungary, the *Yorkshire Post* Shoebox Appeal, and to individuals from Eastern Europe coming to Bible College in England.

Journalists are frequently portrayed as 'enemies' but they themselves often get a bad press. On the whole, I found them to be a bunch of ordinary people who did their job well and in a sensitive way. I would like to think that some have become personal friends. Our local newspapers, the *Telegraph and Argus* and *Shipley Target*, have some intrepid reporters! Their coverage of the whole episode was extensive, to say the least. Over the weeks and months, I had many dealings with Ian Lewis, who was a credit to his profession. His sense of humour was a perfect match for my own, which I had not lost despite the tragic circumstances. I felt I had to write a personal word of thanks to his editor, Perry Austin-Clarke. I told him how the family appreciated the sensitivity of the reporters and photographers, who respected our situation and gave us the 'space' we needed to recover.

One reason I was willing to agree to interviews was that so often I have heard something of interest on the news or in the paper only to find that the item disappears without the final outcome being covered. It's so frustrating. I suppose I'm also very nosey! The other reason was that we have received so much love, care and concern, and people have followed our story with so much interest that I felt I had to continue to the end for their sake. Elizabeth Grice came to interview me on behalf of *The Daily Telegraph*. She wrote an excellent article for the magazine, giving a very good, fair report, covering events in Hungary. This talented journalist ventured north to visit me twice. I trust that we will always be friends, even if she did refer to me as 'chatty, outgoing - reminiscent of a matronly Raymond Briggs character with bright pink cheeks and straight hair'.

The story seemed to run on endlessly in the columns of so many newspapers, encompassing the whole spectrum, including the British dailies, the locals, the *News of the World*, the *Yorkshire Post*, the *New Zealand Herald* - even *Bella* and *The Big Issue*! The family scrapbook began to bulge. Perhaps collecting the cuttings provided a practical diversion for me and the children, during what was a pretty stressful time, as we came to terms with losing a husband and a father. Featured alongside my story in *Best* magazine were 'Curry in a hurry' and 'Why vodka and onions can make you beautiful'. (I definitely didn't fancy the latter, preferring instead the wonderful makeover *Best* treated me to at one of those amazing 'health farms' - unfortunately it didn't last for ever, but I have the photos to prove it wasn't a dream!) I was kindly invited to be a guest of BBC Radio Leeds, twice on the afternoon programme 'Real Lives' and to be interviewed by Peter Levi. Other requests came from Danni Hewson at Pulse Independent Radio, Bradford and others. Later, when I returned to the site of Michael's murder in Nyiregyhaza, I was involved in the making of documentaries with Hungarian TV crews, Yorkshire Television and Mark Brealey from Radio Leeds. For someone not used to all the paraphernalia that goes with broadcasting, it was a bit daunting, to say the least.

The programme 'Kilroy' gave me a powerful insight into the less glamorous side of being involved with the media or being in the full glare of publicity. I had to run the gauntlet of two very angry members of the public who were bitter about their own circumstances and vented their feelings on me. I felt so sorry for them and longed that they could find the inner peace that I knew. I understood how they were hurting. I was too. But being able to forgive was taking away some of the sting of the hurting so that I in turn might not hurt others by being bitter. Again I have to admit that this was not of myself for me to boast in but rather the work of God's Holy Spirit or a special gift of God for that difficult time.

14

The funeral

A time to mourn. (Ecclesiastes 3:4)

The day before the funeral I suffered a flashback to the night of the murder. I was lying in bed, wide awake. There were the usual sounds - the hum of the refrigerator, an occasional passing car, and my cat, Sammy, moving about the house. There was nothing remotely sinister in what I could see or hear, yet, into my mind came thoughts that were totally irrational and unwanted.

'Has someone come to get me? . . . 'Perhaps the men have sent somebody to finish me off as they didn't manage to kill me!'

However unreasonable, these thoughts were very real and very painful. When morning came I found that my fears were unfounded. I was safe. But a long, difficult day lay ahead for us as a family. I knew that, although it would be hard for us, Michael's funeral would have to be public in some way, since his life and death had touched a chord in so many lives. We realized that the day would be shared with the TV and press who still wanted to cover the story.

On 27 August we gathered with family and friends at Nab Wood Crematorium, Shipley, for a service of committal. It was to be followed by a memorial service at City Evangelical Church near Elland Road football ground, Leeds. We had been members of the church years ago when it was located in the city centre and it could hold far more people than the crematorium. But when I arrived at the crematorium, I was overwhelmed by the numbers who had gathered to pay their last respects to Michael; touched also when the policeman who had been on duty directing the cars as we arrived changed out of his uniform into ordinary clothes to attend the service. What with the crowds and the TV camera crews and reporters, the whole scenario was hard to take in and I nearly burst into tears. We had been just such an ordinary couple and yet what had happened had touched many hearts and lives. We were overwhelmed also by the way people had come from far and wide to be with us at both services. Some had travelled great distances, including Tadeuz Tolwinski from Poland. He was quoted by Caroline Cook in the *Yorkshire Post*: 'He was one of my best friends and when I heard about the tragedy, I decided to come to England. We will miss him.'

I was grateful to Professor Verna Wright, the eminent rheumatologist and well-known Christian who married us in 1969, for agreeing to lead the service despite being seriously ill with cancer. He died not many months after Michael. Tributes were given by friends and Roger Carswell gave the address. Many times I had sung solos and organized choirs. Now I felt I should give a personal, final tribute to my husband at the funeral service by singing his favourite hymn, 'How great thou art'. (Interestingly, it had been translated into English and written in part by Stuart Hine [1899-1989] who, with his wife, was a missionary to Eastern Europe. We never met the Hines, but we shared a similar concern for the people of the Ukraine, where he and his wife had worked.) I was sure I could get through all the verses but the congregation was asked to come to my aid should I falter. Roger Carswell, a personal family friend and also an evangelist, found the moment 'unforgettable'. As for Michael, I suspect he would have been amazed at the turnout and wondered what 'all the fuss' was about. The family placed an advert in the local paper thanking the people of Baildon, Shipley and Bradford and beyond for their messages of sympathy, the beautiful flowers and the monetary gifts.

Lifted by the immense love and care shown by so many on that special day, we returned home, where we faced the prospect of having eventually to travel to Hungary for the trial.

15

The trial

Love your enemies. (Matthew 5:4)

I was very apprehensive about the trial. Having to stand in a court of law was intimidating enough of itself. I would be facing the accused and not understanding much of the proceedings, which would be in Hungarian. Within hours of my statement in hospital three men had been arrested: Istvan Dudas, Attila Bilecz and Laszlo Mester. The 'receipts' that the ringleader had handed over to us proved to be speeding tickets issued to one of the gang and their names and addresses were actually on the papers! Their haul was also recovered - £50, two cameras, a microwave, some bread-mix. They had also taken the life of a husband and father.

A copy of the statement I made from my hospital bed had been posted to me. My translator, a man from Derby, had some queries about parts of the police report. It was vitally important to check the statement so that it would be as accurate as possible, with no possible mis-understandings caused by the translation. Rebecca had contacted the Hungarian Embassy staff, who translated the statement into English for me. It contained some sur-prises. Apparently I had said that the men had broken the bathroom door. I couldn't remember saying that, but when the family went to investigate the vehicle they told me that the bathroom door had indeed been ripped off. I was also supposed to have given the men's height in centimetres, which at first seemed strange as I still think in feet and inches! But I felt that when looking at my statement, which was recorded not long after my attack, the court would be bound to take into consideration the terrible head injuries I had suffered. All the same, the statement still caused a nagging worry in my mind as the trial approached.

Rebecca had travelled with me and - like each of the children - was a great support. The three young men had given their statements on December 12. Fortunately, it hadn't been necessary for us be there on that occasion. We flew into Hungary on January 19 so that I could give evidence in the court at Nyiregyhaza on the 23rd. We flew earlier than necessary because I wanted to get the feel of the country - the language, food, atmosphere and people - before going to Nyiregyhaza. The British Embassy had very kindly sent one of their cars to meet us at the airport, to take us on the last lap of the journey to Nyiregyhaza. The driver wasted no time; he fairly flew along those roads, but we all arrived safely and on time! Mandy, the proconsul, accompanied us to our hotel. Also travelling with us was Akos, a Hungarian friend who speaks beautiful English, and was educated in Britain at Southampton University. There he had met our friend, Roger Carswell, and had become a Christian. Akos, who is quite a character, was a great help.

We were scheduled to meet the senior judge at 8.15 a.m., fifteen minutes before the start of the trial. As Rebecca and I walked from the privacy of our hotel room to the court building, we had to run the gauntlet of journalists, cameramen and the whole media circus from various countries, taking pictures and asking questions. I had had no idea what it would be like. It seemed very surreal - the sort of thing I had seen only on television. I had no idea what to do when giving interviews and, to be honest, the whole thing frightened me. With my head down, I held very tightly to the handrail by the steps, and walked slowly into the courtroom.

The room was plain and quite small, but very, very full. Mandy, the proconsul, showed us to our places. Her calm and reassuring presence helped to settle a few nerves, but not all. When the three accused came in, each handcuffed to a prison warder and to each other, I tried not to look them straight in the eye but glanced away. It was the most daunting experience of my life. While giving my statement, with the aid of an interpreter, I was on my feet for an hour and a half. The senior judge, Dr Bodnar Zsolt, seemed a lovely man. He was extremely gentle with his questioning, which I appreciated.

There were queries about several points which did not tally with the original statements I had made when I was first admitted to hospital, and on the evening before my return to England. When my statements were translated back into English, I had found many discrepancies. Rebecca and I had written a 'correct version', which I had circulated to the Embassy, the Foreign and Commonwealth Office, and elsewhere. We thought the judge had received a copy, but maybe he hadn't - hence the long questioning. I felt very anxious lest people would think I was lying. I believed I was telling the truth, but was worried by what the judge would think. I felt like throwing in the towel. However, the judge took everything in his stride and carried on. The defence solicitors, who were sitting quite near to me, not far from the three judges, questioned me too. The first, a man, had a very professional approach. The second, a woman, would have made an excellent border guard in the days of Communism. The third lawyer was also a woman, but she smiled! Her attitude was very positive. It was not the first time that I had seen her, as she had visited me in hospital to ask me if I could say anything good about the three young men. At that time I felt unable to say anything, because I was still coming to terms with the fact that through them Michael had died. She had accepted my response and didn't pursue the matter.

The court was adjourned for a short break so that I could have a drink of water. Being diabetic, I hoped I could withstand the rigours of the long day; after the break I was allowed to remain seated. The trial continued with questions and statements from the prosecutors, judge, doctor and defence lawyers. The doctor was most helpful in sorting out various matters of health concerning the case. He was also able to answer some of the questions about my own physical injuries that were still churning in my head. I had believed that the narcotics sprayed into my face and eyes had acted like an anaesthetic because I didn't feel anything when I was attacked. In fact, I had been knocked unconscious by a heavy kick before being knocked about and beaten up. The doctor said that my memory was impaired and it would take a long time to right itself; there was a certain amount of brain damage, which would also take time to heal. Apparently, when I made my statements I had been lapsing in and out of consciousness, which accounted for the discrepancies. Thankfully, the judge took this into consideration. The stated cause of Michael's death was suffocation; he had drowned in his own blood when his nose was broken.

During the proceedings I was asked to identify which of the three men had 'fined' us for our alleged illegal parking. I had no difficulty in doing so. Later I was asked to identify the man who had broken through the window and caused Michael's death and this was not so easy. While in hospital, I had been shown a photograph of a man all in black. I thought he was the man who had come through the window, so when I saw him in court I identified him as the man in the photograph. The third man I saw for the first time at the trial. I was panicking inside - what if I accused the wrong man? I just didn't know - it was horrible. Later, I was to learn that the man who had fined us was the same man who had come through the window. When he fined us he was wearing a fawn-coloured outfit. He had then returned home and changed into black clothes, intending to disguise himself so I couldn't recognize him. In that he succeeded. I discovered later that he was also the one who had beaten me up.

Towards the end of the afternoon, the judge asked me if I had anything to say to the accused. I wondered what on earth I would say. I hesitated, but then I thought, 'If I can stand up in Britain and say I bear them no malice and have forgiven them and am praying for God to save them, why shouldn't I say it to their face?'

So I did. I replied, 'I have forgiven them.'

Although I didn't look at them properly to start with, I knew that Istvan, Atilla and Laszlo could not do anything to me there in the room. They could not harm me but it was not a happy experience. I said I felt sorry for them because they had ruined their own lives and had prison sentences to face. Yes, they had robbed me of my husband and the children of their father. But as Christians, we knew where Michael was and had the assurance that we would meet again. I told them that I was praying for them, that they too would become Christians and experience God's forgiveness and peace. I told them of the peace I had and the fact that I had no anger. I was able to tell their parents that as a parent myself I had sympathy for them. How they must be devastated by their sons' crimes!

The judges asked the accused if they wanted to speak to me. The young man I had seen for the first time that day said, 'I am so sorry that your children have no father, and that you have lost your husband, I am sorry.' The 'border guard' lawyer told her client to say nothing. The man who was the main protagonist said, 'I have already met a missionary and while I am in prison, I want to learn about the Lord Jesus.'

The court adjourned at about three o'clock. The senior judge asked that I should meet him in an adjoining room to collect my travelling expenses. As he took my hand he said, 'Here I stand . . .' I looked at him, rather puzzled. When he repeated the words the penny dropped. He was quoting Martin Luther's words when he faced his accusers at the Diet of Worms, 'Here I stand, I can do no other.' I realized that although he did not speak English the judge had learned that phrase in order to let me know that he too was a Christian. Mandy from the Embassy told us that we had been invited to go to a children's home for a meal once the court adjourned. On our way there, she told us that this had been the judge's idea. He had contacted the Embassy to say that as it would be a harrowing day for me, at the end of the hearing I needed to do something completely different to take my mind off the day's trauma and so he had arranged this for us. What a man - and how grateful I was for his wisdom! God is so good. We enjoyed both our meal and the visit to see the children. We then returned to Budapest and left for home on January 25.

The following day, I was admitted to hospital in Bradford for attention to an abscess on my chin which had defeated a doctor, a dentist and an orthodontist. The plate in my jaw which was causing the problem had to be removed. Some of the screws had worked loose; one of them was pushing its way from inside my mouth through to the outside. Besides the pain there was a lot of pus and blood; it was not a pretty sight for the squeamish. Once the plate was removed, the infection disappeared, but I still required further surgery at a later stage.

The young men were sentenced on Friday, February 6. Istvan Dudas, who had caused Michael's death, received an eleven-year sentence - he was only eighteen when he committed the crime. The second man, Attila Bilecz, aged twenty-two, received a seven-year sentence. Laszlo Mester, also aged twenty-two, was jailed for six years. All three defendants appealed against their sentences, so I had to return to Hungary on June 3, 1998. Again, I had to relive those awful memories of the attack. At the appeal trial at the Supreme Court, I met the parents of Dudas and some of his relatives. It was a desperately sad situation; his father seemed a broken man. I went to him, put my arms around him and wept with him. After meeting Dudas' mother and relatives also, I feel that we have become friends. The poignancy of the fact that Dudas is just twelve days younger than my son, Andrew, did not escape my notice. 'There but for the grace of God go I.'

16

In prison

I was in prison and you
came to visit me.
(Matthew 25:36)

Istvan Dudas shares a tiny cell with other inmates. There is a toilet and a table and each man has a locker and a bed. Prisoners have to wash their clothes in their cells, by hand. In another part of the prison, I gather that twenty-five men have to share a room. Dudas may be given work constructing the sports hall. Conditions are extremely spartan. The prison sentence will be no joy-ride.

At the end of the interview for Yorkshire Television, I said from my hospital bed that I bore no malice to the men. This surprised people - and me too, because previously I hadn't really thought how I felt. But the more I reflected on it, the more convinced I was that although I don't like what they did, and wish it had never happened, I didn't hate them. I miss Michael dreadfully and feel very lonely without him. It is such a comfort to know that God never makes mistakes. I know where Michael is, and that one day I'll see him again. I know that Michael would have wanted people to pray that the men will find Jesus as their Saviour, even in prison.

Letters to my attackers

Shipley, West Yorkshire, England

Dear Laszlo,

I am writing to you to tell you that I often think of you, and wonder how you are. I was very sorry that I didn't see you last year when I came to visit the three of you in Budapest. I wanted to make sure that you knew that I have truly forgiven all of you, and that I love each one of you. When I saw you in the court in Nyiregyhaza I felt I wanted to bring you back home and 'straighten you out'!!!

I was very sad to discover that your parents are both dead. Do you have any brothers and sisters? If you have, I hope they visit you as often as they can. Did you receive the gift I sent you? I hope it was useful to you. I hope you have the opportunity to learn English while in prison. You have a very good accent.

It is almost Christmas and I know it will be a difficult time for you and your family. We will be praying for you, that God will give you his LOVE, JOY and PEACE.

I have sent you some Christian books in Hungarian to read. If you do not want to read them, please do not destroy them. Instead, please would you give them to another prisoner who would like to read them, or to the prison chaplain.

I want to come back to Hungary to see how each of you are and I hope you will be able to meet me when I come. Remember that I have forgiven you, but better still, God will forgive you if you tell him that you are truly sorry for wrong things you have done in your life.

He Loves YOU!

Shipley, West Yorkshire, England

Dear Istvan,

It is a long time since I heard from you. In fact it was a year ago. I wrote to you when I returned from New Zealand, but did not receive a reply. I wondered if your friend, who translated our letters, had moved to a different cell or had completed his sentence. My problem was because I know very little Hungarian!

However, there is a young Hungarian lady who lives about ten minutes away from me, and she is willing to translate our letters. There is another Hungarian lady living eight kilometers away, and she too, will help. Her husband drives to Hungary sometimes, and he has said I could travel with them sometime. I really do want to return to Hungary to visit you and your parents, and my other friends. Please give your parents my love and best wishes, and your two aunts too.

Do you still enjoy the Bible Studies and the service on a Sunday? I have some Hungarian books which I will send you from time to time. If you don't want to read them, please do not destroy them, but pass them on to someone else who would appreciate them, or to the prison chaplain.

It is almost Christmas, and it will be a difficult time for you and your parents, but we will be praying for you all, and hoping that you will experience the love of God. My forgiveness remains, as does my love for you, and I hope that you will be willing to let me visit you again, without all the media-hype.

May God help you and give you His peace and love day by day.

Shipley, West Yorkshire, England

Dear Attila,

I am writing to tell you that I haven't forgotten you. Thank you for meeting me in the prison in Budapest. I know that it must have been difficult for you both, especially with all the media who were there. I knew that there was a cameraman for the BBC, but was surprised by all the others who were there. I am sorry if it caused you any embarrassment.

The reason for my visit was to meet you and make sure that you knew that I have truly forgiven all three of you, and that I love you all. I am a Christian, and it is Jesus who has given me this love and forgiveness. He will forgive you too, if you tell Him you are really sorry for the wrong things you have done. He loves you and died for you.

I am sending you some Christian books, which are in Hungarian. I would like you to read them, but if you don't want to, please do not destroy them. You could give them to another prisoner, who will read them, or to the prison chaplain.

I would be very happy, if you wrote to me from time to time. The days must drag by in prison. Do you have a job there?

Do you have brothers and sisters? And are your parents both alive? It is almost Christmas, and I know it will be a difficult time for you and your relatives. I shall be thinking about you, and praying for you.

May you know the LOVE and PEACE of God.

17

Grief

Grief itself is a medicine.[7]

What a friend we have in Jesus,
All our sins and griefs to bear;
What a privilege to carry everything to God in prayer[8]

Losing a loved one is hard at any age. I do not pretend to be an authority on grief, though I have lost both my parents and husband and other relatives. I can only share my experience in the hope that it may touch a chord with someone or explain why I can smile, in spite of great personal loss and injury.

For each person the situation and how he or she copes is different. We all have our own ways of expressing those deep inner personal feelings which hurt so much. Some react to death by emotionally moving no further than the land of *If Only*, where bitterness and regret seem to grow. Another natural reaction is to defuse grief by finding someone or something *to blame*, especially if the cause of death is unnatural. Some have found comfort in having *friends to talk with*, yet others find solace in the quiet presence of *someone who says nothing* but imparts inner strength at just the right time. I know that when I cried to God in the van at my point of deepest hurt, he heard and answered. Your hurt may be a very different kind, the inner anguish known only to God, yet he will answer even the faintest whisper of someone who needs him and wants him.

I couldn't put on an act. Publicly, I was not grieving with an outward show of emotion. I think that throughout the whole ghastly experience I was on autopilot. It wasn't until I came back from a trip to New Zealand in 1998 with Rebecca that I really began to grieve in private, but then it came with a vengeance. Knowing how long it had taken me to break down after my mother's death, I suspected I would suffer a similar long delay after losing Michael.

There are many books on the subject of grief, which can be of help in those times of trouble and heartbreak. In Warren Wiersbe's booklet, *Jesus and your Sorrows*, he emphasizes that the initial step in grief is to accept our sorrow, while expressing it naturally. Then, be patient with yourself, giving yourself time to heal. Accept the help that friends and family give. Allow them to help in practical ways. God uses people to encourage and help us during the dark days of grief.

Reading some of the promises of God in the Bible really helped me, both straight after the attack, and daily, as the whole ghastly effects of the brutal episode unfolded.

Doctors often refer to 'the stages in grieving', all of which are part of the healing process. Of course, there is the initial shock. It is then that all the inevitable questions, often beginning with the word, 'why?', come to our minds so quickly.

Sometimes immediately, sometimes days or weeks later, our emotions seem to take over. Tears tumble. We mourn and weep. This time of outward hurting may be followed by a time of depression and loneliness. Some people feel actual physical pain. Some experience pangs of guilt or even anger against God. Wiersbe says that this is quite normal, so we do not need to be afraid.'

> 'Slowly we regain our perspective and learn to accept reality. Our hearts still hurt, but now we are able to handle it, and receive strength from the Lord . . . We will never forget the past, nor should we try to forget . . . The tendency to capture the past and hold it prisoner is not the Christian approach to life. . . We cannot change the past; but if we are not careful we can be chained to the past . . . Memories become rudders to guide us, not anchors to hold us back.'

I know that I cannot change the past, but I can change how the past influences me. My tomorrow is in God's hand, just as was the night of August 4, 1997. I need not fear the future, for my Lord, whom I love and serve, is 'the God who doesn't make mistakes'.

18

Memorial

As time passed, events unfolded, putting into place the final pieces of the tragic jigsaw of an aid trip 'gone wrong'. There was an inquest in Bradford. Mr Whittaker, the coroner, said that Michael had suffered 34 injuries to his face and head, and that he had died after inhaling blood and suffering a heart attack. The jury returned a verdict of unlawful killing.

Meanwhile, in Nyiregyhaza, a Hungarian newspaper reported on the local response to the fateful event in their town:

> Almost one year has passed since the still incomprehensible tragic death of British Pastor Michael Trevor Pollard. The Hungarian Democratic Forum (MDF) and the Pollard Commemorative Committee will erect a memorial (a carved wooden post) on the site of the shocking event on Sunday April 19 at 10 a.m. First Ferenc Petróczki, president of the county chapter of the MDF, will address the audience, then Dr József Zilahi, chairman of the county general assembly, will recount what happened a year ago. After a speech by Sándor Lezsák, president of the MDF, participants will take part in an ecumenical service to pay tribute to the pastor. It is the intention of the Commemorative Committee that the memorial serve as a memento to all well-intentioned people longing for security and denounc-

ing the brutality and violence increasingly widespread these days.

Inevitably, I had to return one day to the actual place where we were attacked. My last recollections of it were all in the dark, literally, as it had happened in the night. At Dover one of France's notorious strikes meant that we were held up for ages. There, right in front of us as we queued, was a lorry from Hungary. 'How ironic!' I thought. On closer examination, it actually came from Nyiregyhaza, where we were ambushed!

I naturally felt apprehensive about the trip, which I realized might offer an opportunity to face the issue of standing again on the very spot where Michael had died. I would not have been happy or felt safe going on my own. It was planned to be only a short trip and I had contacted the Mayor of Nyiregyhaza to ask him if he could help me to do the things I had in mind. He proved to be brilliant and organized everything I had asked for.

To visit the hospital was a number one priority, to show them how well I looked, but also to thank them. It was good to meet again the Christian doctor who had been so kind to me and provided accommodation for two of my children every night. The outing to the children's home was a wonderful experience. I love children very much. The art-craft items I had taken for them were much appreciated because they enjoy drawing so much and making murals. I had hoped to meet one of the judges, but he was abroad at the time. Another interesting reunion was with the policeman who worked so hard last year catching the young men. He, too, was on holiday with his parents but came back especially to meet me.

Our party was wonderfully welcomed at the county council headquarters, where we enjoyed a five-course meal before going to visit the parents of Istvan Dudas, the main protagonist. I learned that the family was very poor and relied on selling their chickens and eggs. Having previously met the parents at the Supreme Court in June and established a friendship, I wanted to give some practical help. The events had almost broken Istvan's father. Ostracized by the neighbours, he and his wife find life very difficult. Once a month one of them sets off at three or four o'clock in the morning to catch the train to Budapest, from where they then have to walk some distance to the prison. They get back home at about 11 p.m. Istvan is their only child. His 94-year-old grandmother will probably never see him again.

I offered to meet Attila's parents but they chose not to, for whatever reason. The brothers and sisters of Laszlo Mester, who is an orphan, also declined. However I left each family some Yorkshire tea and a tea towel with pictures of the Yorkshire Dales. Mr Dudas said he would deliver them.

When the time came for me to visit two of the men in a Budapest prison, feelings of apprehension returned. It is quite daunting to enter a penal institution, let alone meet prisoners. When I was introduced to the men, without really considering the implications of such an action, I greeted them in the European way, with kisses on the cheeks. Cameras flashed. Quite unintentionally, I had sparked off a whole new set of headlines such as, 'A Kiss for Killer' and 'Widow's Kiss says she has Forgiven'. I was with them for twenty minutes during which time they apologized to me. They said that things had not gone the way they had intended and that they were sorry for Michael's death. One of them gave me something he had made for me in prison. I gave each of them a toiletry bag containing soap, shampoo and toothpaste as a practical symbol of forgiveness. Both said they would like me to visit them again. The prison authorities felt it was a positive visit. It was the first time anyone had made a request to visit the killers of a relative.

The night before I actually went to Nyiregyhaza, it was hard to sleep. The next day, at the beautiful memorial set up by the local people near the lay-by, I scattered rose petals from our garden back in England. Then I sang a hymn, the same one that we had at our wedding and that I had sung also at the funeral. The whole trip was quite emotionally charged.

But I'm so glad I went. It was the last place Michael and I were together. Although I believe that when he died he went straight to be with God, and his body had been cremated, this was an opportunity for me to 'say' my final goodbye to him.

19

Aftermath and re-entry

We are an ordinary family, who have been allowed to drink from life's cup, which, for us, was mixed with extraordinary adventures and opportunities, laced with risk and danger.

As for myself, I've been beaten up and survived. I'm retired. I've lost my husband. (But Vance Havner says you don't lose someone when you know where they are.) The children are flying from the nest, so what in the world is there left for me now? 'Normal' life now beckons - whatever that may mean!

Michael would have been proud to see what the children have achieved. *Rebecca* was awarded a diploma in computing, with the highest grade possible, at Leeds Metropolitan University. She successfully completed courses in photography and computer graphics; currently she designs and implements the web-site for a legal software house. *Tamar* gained her degree and PGCE before starting her first job as a teacher in Chesterfield. *Andrew* gained four A Level passes (three at grade A) before leaving home for Nottingham University. Each in their own way has supported and helped me to face the future.

As I write this, I realize I am still on my path of recovery. Although my diabetes is stable and my jaw and face have healed, I have some memory problems. A blood clot which was present in my brain after the attack has apparently dissolved. I had a brain scan, underwent further tests, and was seen by a neurologist. It is felt that some of my memory loss may be due to the grieving process.

I shall never forget my first excursion back into the land of normality, when I visited my local supermarket. Rebecca accompanied me to Asda to help with choosing and transporting the groceries. For the first time in my life somebody called me 'that woman'! An old couple were pushing their trolley past me when the lady spotted me. All of a sudden she cried out loudly, 'It's that woman!' With that, they scuttled off before I could catch them. I just wanted to say, 'Thank you for recognizing me. God bless you.' No doubt they didn't know what to say or were embarrassed. So it happened that to many people I became 'that woman', who had been on TV or in the paper. While I was in hospital I had received a card from all the friends at Asda. It is such a friendly supermarket where every week I meet or make friends with someone or other, which all helps in my recovery.

The *Telegraph and Argus* reported another important stage in my path of recovery. In March 1998 I made my first aid mission to Europe since the tragedy, travelling to Latvia and Lithuania with Aid to the Baltic Communities, a Doncaster-based group made up of local church members. I was invited to speak to two churches in the Doncaster area on the date of what would have been our twenty-ninth wedding anniversary. I also sang the hymn 'How great thou art'. It's a hymn that means a lot to me; it's part of me and was part of our life together. It was our wedding hymn. We have sung it together in Eastern Europe. We also sang it at Tamar's baptism. And it was the hymn that I tried out when I was in hospital after the attack, wondering whether I could still sing with a broken jaw!

I wanted to get back as soon as I could to help with the choir at my former school. However, on the day I had planned to return to assist them, I discovered that choir practice had been cancelled. It was the first time I had been back into school since Michael's death. I went outside and there was my old class waiting to go into lunch. They chatted away to me about Michael and his death. Being with the children was the best therapy for me. They said they had prayed for me and spoke openly about the details of what had happened. It made the whole business of my re-entry into normal life so much easier.

My days of travelling across Europe by camper van are over. But I keep in contact with the hundreds of friends made over thirty years. I have entered the world of technology and discovered e-mail. There are so many needs around the world and in our neighbourhoods, so many prayers to be prayed, causes to support, burdens to share, kind words to say that I guess none of us need ever be idle. I have found, too, that we are never alone if God is in our hearts.

Postscript

Over the years, it never entered my head to even think of writing a book. My family and friends in New Zealand and Australia will confirm that I am a dreadful correspondent and seldom put pen to paper, but experiences in different countries and situations gave Michael and me an unusual perspective on life. We were both teachers and therefore interested in the surroundings, history, folklore and people. We were also committed Christians and believed in the Jesus of the Bible, so we were travelling with a purpose with and for the Lord. He never let us down and never makes mistakes. And writing a book was not a new idea.

Before we set off on our travels in 1997, Michael and I had made three decisions. The first was to sell the motor home. After the Hungarian police had finished checking out the motor home in which my dear husband had been murdered, I was unsure what to do with it. So much of our lives had been connected with the van and, apart from the practical questions, having to cope with selling it was emotionally draining. As the vehicle itself had been damaged in the attack, it was put to me that perhaps, rather than sell it, it might be wiser to scrap it altogether. This is what we did. To my great relief, I never had to go inside the van again.

Our second decision was to visit my family in New Zealand and Australia; Rebecca and I made the trip in 1998.

The third decision we made before going on our last trip - and the most daunting one - was to write a book about our work in Eastern Europe. Like the others, it was intended to be achieved in the company of Michael and I know that he would have wanted me to have a go at writing the book. Now all three decisions have been accomplished with the support of family and friends. So this is the book. I hope that I have done justice to Michael's memory.

(If you would like a free copy of the booklet 'Comfort in Sorrow' or other Christian literature please contact Jo Pollard, c/o Paternoster Publishing, PO Box 300, Kingstown Broadway, Carlisle, Cumbria, CA3 0QS.
Or e-mail: carswell77@aol.com)

Lives of great men all remind us we can make
our lives sublime
And departing leave behind us footprints on
the sand of time

Tributes

Some of the following tributes were received at the funeral. Some were personal letters. The first four are by Rebecca, Tamar and Andrew

My Dad

My Dad is an elderly man
He has faded blue eyes covered by a pair of new bifocal glasses
His nose is on the large side and his lips are thin like a runner bean
He has hairy arms and legs like a monkey's
He has wavy greyish-black hair
He can be very stern, mean and stern as a mule
But often he is nice, kind but silly
He runs about singing ridiculous songs
He has a peculiar character

REBECCA POLLARD September 1984

My Dad

Blue socks
Brown trousers
Grey cotton
Two paces stroll in front of the family
Was it because he was always late?
Work - family rugby as well as the Lord
He certainly tried

Driven in all he did
Sometimes driving us mad
His guidance came from above
His enthusiasm relentless

Donating his life to others
Made many think him strange
And often decided to mock
But he knew that God was on his side
And prayed that the persecutors would join the flock

His death came sudden
But these things happen in our family
So I was not shocked
I know he is now in safe hands

Maybe others learning of his cause
Will also now one-day end up with the Lord

REBECCA POLLARD *(10 September 2000)*

TAMAR'S TRIBUTE

It's hard to know where to begin when I reflect on Dad as there's so much I could say, so many memories I could share. As I've sifted through and tried to select, I've been reminded of Proverbs 17:6 where it says that the pride of children is their father. How true that is for me, for all of us Pollard children, for regardless of his failings and flaws, Dad was a father we could be proud of, his humility and compassion, all that he accomplished in his quiet, unassuming way. What an example he set and what support he provided. He was, and is, indeed, the pride of his children.

Among my early memories I recall an untidy man, who despite being constantly on the move, still found the time to sit with me upon his knee and make up silly, untuneful songs. More importantly he would find time daily to read the Bible with me and pray. I can still clearly picture him sitting on my bed helping and encouraging me, and then tenderly bidding me goodnight. I learnt so much about the Christian life through those times and really value the training Dad gave me - not just then but also later on when he took me along to all sorts of events, sent me on camps and missions and encouraged me to be as much involved as possible - much like he already did.

During the two years when I attended the school where he taught I sometimes felt embarrassed at his unkempt appearance, poor dress sense and appalling time-keeping. I also began to resent the fact that my popularity was affected by his Christian beliefs. Nevertheless I often loved the fact I was Mr. Pollard's daughter, as so many of the pupils loved and respected him. He was seen as gentle and fair, and as one who rarely lost his temper (the same was true at home). The Good News Club he ran used to attract over 70 pupils each meeting and I remember meeting for prayer with other pupils on a regular basis. I certainly couldn't even hazard a guess how many young people Dad helped spiritually, but many were certainly influenced through his work in school, Young Life and church.

I've already mentioned how Dad's appearance and lack of punctuality embarrassed me. A further illustration is the fact that on many occasions when I was at Bradford Girls' Grammar School. I used to get so frustrated by him that, vainly hoping he would be on time, I would tell him to collect me half an hour earlier than was really necessary. For a while I used to ask him to collect me from the school gate because I was embarrassed by the Skoda he drove and the clothes he wore. Then one day I was hit by the thought that dad dressed as he did because he had greater priorities, and drove the car he did, so that he could spend and give his money elsewhere. As I saw my Dad practising what he preached it really challenged my thinking and value system. He lived selflessly and sacrificially for the honour of his Saviour. My teenage years were further influenced by seeing Dad each morning sitting up in his bed surrounded by his Bible, Daily Light, prayer letters and his copy of the Operation World prayer guide. Both at the beginning and the end of each day he gave time to commune with his Lord, to grow in knowledge and understanding, and to intercede for those more needy than himself. Dad was who he was because of these times - and of course the grace of God.

As I grew older I seemed to grow closer and closer to Dad. We had so many shared interests, from sport to history, and of course our faith. I spent so much time with him, both at rugby matches, where he'd meticulously record every incident or goal and also at Christian meetings. He encouraged and enthused me to get involved, to investigate and explore, to persevere, in a huge range of things. He became one of my closest friends, a loyal supporter and a much needed wise advisor. I discussed anything and everything with him, knowing he would listen with open ears, a caring heart, and a sound mind. Even when I went to university, I would be able to ring at any time, day or night, and chat and pray things through over the phone.

Dad was a man who loved a hug; he used to cry each time he dropped me off at university and said goodbye. A man also who frustrated and often neglected his family in his attempt to juggle his many commitments. Dad was someone whose sacrificial and focused living was, and is, a constant challenge to me - and to others. Dad, who died a death allowed by God, used by God and is now in heaven alongside God. Dad was not just 'someone' - he was my Dad whom I loved very much and miss greatly. Dad was so special, words do not do him justice.

TAMAR POLLARD *(January 2001)*

ANDREW'S TRIBUTE

Four situations spring to mind that summarize the fond memories of my father. Firstly, I can remember the times when I had tests at school such as spelling, geography, French etc. After revising the test-material, my father was always pleased to test me. Some people might find this boring but I used to enjoy trying to impress him by doing my best to get all the answers correct: this was certainly a great help in the tests themselves! Often he would ask questions related to the subject that were not actually to be tested and these were the questions I tried hardest to answer. I have found his broad general knowledge and enthusiasm as a teacher a great inspiration, especially in my academic career.

I also remember fondly the Leeds rugby league games I would attend with my father, watching them play both home and away. I particularly enjoyed sharing the atmosphere and excitement of the games and liked to read and annotate the match programmes with him. As well as the games themselves I also looked forward to the journeys to and from the matches when my father would entertain me with anecdotes about going to the rugby games when he was my age.

Besides being interested in rugby, my father was also a keen cricket fan and in the summer would recruit a cricket team to go and play the young men at the Assessment Centre at the end of our road. The youths in the centre were generally well behaved and enjoyed playing with us. What I particularly enjoyed about the games were the times when my father and I were either batting partners or fielding in the same region of the pitch. This is because I was never particularly gifted at cricket and was always a little worried about letting the team down, hence, I always felt better when I received the encouragement and advice/instructions he would often give me.

ANDREW POLLARD *(15 January 2001)*

I think he offered children a chance to express themselves in a way not possible at home or at school - with a love, unspoken but inherent in the way he led his life, both then and for the rest of his life. Thinking back, I can see in him the person he was to become in later life. What I am grateful for is that he showed me his love of life and he lived it without hesitation. **Eric Clarkson**: *former pupil at St Phillip's, Burley-in-Wharfedale*.

My contact with Mike after we went abroad was every four or five years when we would come home on furlough. I remember thinking, this is the man who seemed sad and lonely but on holiday was utterly transformed. He was a new creature altogether because of Christ's work in his life. If he simply saw a need or needy people without Christ he was available with what gifts God had given him. When on furlough it was customary for me to speak in their home to all and sundry who could be enticed in. The room was usually too small for all who came. The few chairs were quickly taken and the rest of the people plonked down on the carpet or a chair arm. Many hosts would have squirmed at not being able to make everyone comfortable but Mike and Jo took it in their stride, presumably more focused on the opportunity to share the gospel than logistical issues. Once when we came home to England we discovered that Mike was now the driving force behind a new church in Shipley. He seemed to do everything, including lining up speakers, arranging work parties to upgrade the facilities and promoting future evangelistic events. Mike impressed me as being totally available for the Lord and thus often more effective than others who may have been theoretically more gifted. It goes without saying that God's provision of a good wife and their ability to work as a team was another big factor in their effectiveness for Christ. **Stuart Shepherd:** *friend.*

We both remember Mr Pollard from an early age, walking past the Pollard household and talking to the family as well as the guinea pigs, rabbit and cats.

I (Richard) was the first of the two of us to attend Ladderbanks Middle School, starting there in 1992. Mr Pollard played a big part in my education, teaching me French, Maths, History and Religious Education at various stages in my time at Ladderbanks. This demonstrates just how much of an impact Mr Pollard had on my development from a child to a young adult.

I (Claire) went to Ladderbanks in 1994. Unfortunately I did not have the chance to gain from Mr Pollard's teaching, as he retired during my first year at the school. We were regular members of the Friday lunchtime Good News Club. Here we were give the chance to explore Christianity in a unique way. We participated in various activities, including singing songs, visiting speakers, stories of the Bible, regular issues of Tearaways magazine and fundraising for Tear Fund. Mr Pollard also organized regular trips for members of Good News Club. For both of us the most memorable was a trip to a farm in Hawksworth where - as we vividly remember - we were given the opportunity to hold young lambs. Mr and Mrs Pollard have always been close friends of the family and we were all deeply saddened and shocked to hear of his death and the circumstances surrounding it. **Richard and Claire Limbert:** *former pupils at Ladderbanks School.*

Here at Gargrave Primary we have been shocked and saddened to hear about Mr Pollard's tragic death in Hungary while you were on your way back from your aid mission to Romania. Your husband had been coming to our school every term to take assembly and he often spoke of the people he met in those countries, especially the children, and his eye-witness accounts were very meaningful to our pupils . . . They always looked forward to Mr Pollard's assemblies and remembered afterwards what had been said . . . We will miss him very much. **Edna Mansley:** *Religious Education Co-ordinator, Gargrave Primary School.*

Thousands of believers were blessed by the Bibles they ferried into the Communist countries, and equal numbers have appreciated the humanitarian and spiritual aid they brought after the Iron Curtain crumbled. Michael was an outstanding example of Christian courage, determination and wholehearted love for the Lord. There are people with great natural ability who have not accomplished a quarter of what he did. **Verna Wright:** *Professor of Rheumatology, University of Liverpool, President, Young Life.*

The presence of so many people from all over the British Isles is tribute to all that Michael accomplished. One of the things that amazed me about him was his seeming ordinariness. Yet he did so much. There is a sense in which any Christian could perhaps have done some of the things he did but Mike was determined to do all that he could and so in so many areas he accomplished so much for the Lord. Other people come and go on beach missions, but Mike kept going every year as he could, telling others about the Saviour. Earlier this year he was at Whitby . . . Given the opportunity, Mike did whatever he could. Thus when he moved to Shipley he started a Young Life group in his home; and it was the same in other areas of service. The way that Mike Pollard would see an opportunity and - if no one else did so - would go on with it through and through, is a challenge to us all. His last written communication to us at the UBM office was: 'Christ has given assurance my sins are forgiven, and peace, and I know where I am going when I die.' That was the secret of his life. **Gordon Robertson:** *General Secretary, United Beach Missions.*

I got involved with Mike at the Ladderbanks School Good News Club. It met twice a week at lunch time. One of the three legacies he left us is the number of lives now lived for Jesus Christ that would not have happened were Mike not ministering there. He taught in the school but he also lived his life there. Those pupils knew Mike's life was different.

The second legacy is of someone who cares, shown especially through 'Young Life'. The group was a mixed bunch; it didn't matter who you were or what you were, if you turned up on a Saturday you were made welcome. Mike mirrored the life of Jesus - he spent hours and hours with individuals.

The third legacy is one which he possibly left to me. He was the most untrendy character imaginable. Today's young people would describe him as 'sad'. Mike always had a black book with everything in it, but it used to bother me that he took his glasses off to read it. And they were reading glasses. His absent-mindedness would cause chaos with appointments - he'd be there but not on the right day. He couldn't care less what people thought about him, but he cared dearly what people thought about his Saviour. **A Friend**.

On behalf of those involved in Eastern Europe Ministries, I am grateful for the life and work of Michael Pollard. He was quiet and unassuming, but his determination to touch the church in Eastern Europe has left its mark. When I remember him three words come to mind. They probably sum up all of his life - not just his ministry. The first is *people*. Michael and Jo were both deeply concerned about the situation in Eastern and central Europe. When I met Michael he was passing through Vienna, collecting contact addresses, material and aid and moving out into Europe. People in the suffering church needed to know that the West cared and Michael was one of those who assured them of this. He sorted out specific needs and worked to meet them. The second is *prayer*. Michael's world was bound up with the lives of those who lived in and worked in Eastern Europe. He not only prayed personally but he encouraged many others to become involved. Often he asked for information to fuel the little Albanian prayer group in which he was involved. The third word is *promotion*. Following Michael and Jo's trips there was always the annual bulletin, telling about their journeys and encouraging prayer. Michael also made a multitude of visits to churches around the country, speaking about the needs of Eastern Europe. **Margaret Willan:** *Northern representative, European Christian Mission.*

Then I heard a voice from heaven say, 'Write: Blessed are the dead who die in the Lord from now on.' 'Yes,' says the Spirit, 'they will rest from their labour, for their deeds will follow them.' (Rev. 14:13).This verse shows us how important it is to die in the Lord to be blessed and Michael died in the Lord. Michael will no more travel to Eastern Europe, he will have no more trouble on the border, his works are following him. The works are not in front of him, they follow him. We won't see him in Poland again but we will see him in his work he left in Poland. **Tadeusz Tolwinski:** *Pastor in Torun, Poland.*

Funeral Message

At the crematorium service Roger Carswell spoke from Revelation 21:1-4 (NKJV):

> Now I saw a new heaven and a new earth, for the first heaven and the first earth had passed away. Also there was no more sea. Then I, John, saw the holy city, New Jerusalem, coming down out of heaven from God, prepared as a bride adorned for her husband. And I heard a loud voice from heaven saying, "Behold, the tabernacle of God *is* with men, and He will dwell with them, and they shall be His people. God Himself will be with them *and be* their God. And God will wipe away every tear from their eyes; there shall be no more death, nor sorrow, nor crying. There shall be no more pain, for the former things have passed away."

<u>This is the funeral message he gave later that day at the Thanksgiving Service</u>

As we meet to give thanks for Michael Pollard, we all feel a great sense of loss. This was well expressed by a little lad who went into the local newsagent shortly after Michael's murder and, hearing one of the customers talking about Michael, interrupted and said, 'I don't have many friends, but Mr Pollard was my friend.' Many of us feel that he was a good, good friend. So far about a thousand people have sent cards or letters to the Pollards. But what if the Lord Jesus Christ could have written a letter and sent it directly to Jo and Rebecca and Tamar and Andrew? What would he have said? Like Michael, Jesus died a brutal death. He rose triumphantly from the dead and ascended to heaven. And he dictated seven letters. They were to individual churches; you can read them in the opening chapters of the final book of the Bible. Jo and the family have been greatly encouraged by the cards and letters they have received. They have read them carefully. I suppose millions of words have been spoken throughout the land about Michael Pollard's murder, but what matters most is what God says. What is his estimation of what happened? We have an insight into this, in his letter to the church at Smyrna, which today is called Izmir, and is situated in Turkey.

> "And to the angel of the church in Smyrna write, 'These things says the First and the Last, who was dead, and came to life: "I know your works, tribulation, and poverty (but you are rich); . . Do not fear any of those things which you are about to suffer . . . Be faithful until death, and I will give you the crown of life"' (Revelation 2:8-10 NKJV).

This church had gone through persecution and the people were suffering immensely. They will have been encouraged by the first words of the letter. 'I am the First and the Last.' The words reminded them that Jesus was God clothed in humanity. When the Christians of Smyrna heard those words they heard Christ saying, 'I am in control, I am in charge, nothing ever takes me by surprise, I am never caught out unawares, there never comes a moment when I think, "Oh I wasn't expecting that." I am the first and the last.'

Michael, Jo and the family had proved that truth many times throughout their lives and their ministry. There was the time when they arrived in a large Romanian city, during the Communist period, knowing there were Christian believers there but uncertain how to find them. They committed themselves to God and parked and slept the night in their caravanette. When morning came the tapping they heard at the window proved to be the very man they had come to visit - and outside whose flat they had actually parked. God was in control.

God was in control when the border guard they feared the most was afflicted at the crucial moment with a terrible headache and one of her colleagues waved the Pollards through - God was in control. God was in charge.

Then there was the time when they were turned away at the Romanian border and so went into Hungary. The first couple to give them hospitality had a little child. Michael and Jo asked, 'Could you use any baby food?' and the couple burst into tears and said, 'We have no baby food, we have been praying that God would somehow send it to us.' God was in control.

Notice too that the Lord Jesus Christ also reminded this persecuted church of what he had suffered. 'I am the one who died and came back to life. I have gone through what many of you in Smyrna are going to go through.' To us he says, 'I have gone through what Michael Pollard went through and I came back to life, I have conquered death.'

Then, having introduced himself, he speaks directly to the church about its situation. He has no word of criticism, simply a word of comfort to these suffering Christians. Those words offer comfort to us here and now. 'I know your works,' he says, 'your tribulation and poverty. I know about the troubles you are going through, I know the poverty you are experiencing, I know the opposition you are facing.'

In that church at Smyrna there was a lad called Polycarp. Later he became the leader of the church. When he was an old man thousands of citizens who had crowded into the arena and had seen a number of Christians killed began to shout out 'Polycarp, Polycarp!' He was offered the opportunity to turn from his beliefs and renounce Jesus. His reply was simple: 'Eighty and six years I have served him and he never did me wrong, how can I now speak evil of my King who has saved me?' So they burned the old man alive.

'I know', said the Lord Jesus. God was absolutely aware of all that would happen on what we feel was an ill-fated trip. He went on to say, 'Be faithful, even to the point of death, and I will give you the crown of life.' He is aware of all that will happen to Jo and Rebecca and Tamar and Andrew. He tells them what he told Joshua centuries before: 'I will never leave you nor forsake you'. Your husband, your father may have been taken from you, but God never leaves you. You will never be alone.

The encouragement we have been thinking about so far is comfort for the here and now. But there is also comfort for the long term. God brings triumph out of tragedy, and light out of darkness. The Apostle Paul was sure of this, as he said, that 'Christ will be magnified in my body, whether by life or by death'. Michael, this very moment, is in heaven. But what about those Hungarian young men? Jo has pleaded with us to pray for them. An 18-year-old murdered an innocent worker. They have wrecked their lives - how shattered their families must feel. We must pray that they will be converted and find full and free forgiveness through the Lord Jesus Christ.

We have already reminded ourselves that God brings triumph out of tragedy and light out of darkness. The greatest example of this is the Lord Jesus himself. It is because of his death that those young men can find forgiveness. He came to earth with the express mission of being faithful unto death and going to the cross of Calvary. There he took on himself our sin, your sin, my sin, the sins that would condemn us to hell - he took them on himself. If only we will trust in him, we can be forgiven and - like Michael - be assured of a new life in heaven. It was in order to give us a crown of life that Christ was faithful unto death.

Michael is in heaven. The moment his life was taken from him, the moment he was absent from the body, he was present with the Lord. There are many friends of his there, including Mark, Michael and Jo's own little son, who died in infancy - but best of all, Jesus is there. Michael will be able to gaze on and serve the Lord whom he loved. We need to be quite clear about why Michael is in heaven. It's not because he was a kind man or a generous man, although he was both of these; it's not even because he died in such terrible circumstances. He is in heaven because there came a moment in his life, when, turning from sin in repentance, he trusted Jesus Christ. He asked Christ to be his Lord and Saviour. I know that Michael's greatest desire for each of us would be that we might do the same. You may have lived a religious life for years, or you may have led a very irreligious life, but I would urge you this very afternoon quietly to cry out to God in your heart of hearts and ask him to save you, to forgive you, to come and live within you, to be with you throughout the rest of your life, through death and throughout all eternity.

We can be sure this would have been Michael's greatest desire because of the sacrifices he and Jo made. On the occasion when they were fined at the Romanian border and Jo was held as a hostage they had sufficient funds in their caravanette, but they wouldn't touch that money because it had been given for Christians in Eastern Europe and they would not use it for their own sakes. So they phoned the Building Society and took on an extra mortgage without telling anyone how much they had borrowed. All that money was eventually sent in gifts to Michael and Jo, but the point is, they sought to never abuse the trust people had put in them.

But why were they there? Because they wanted Romanians to hear about the Lord Jesus Christ. When

Michael went to Albania with Arnaldo, a Spanish friend, they knew that the punishment for possessing a Bible in Albania was execution. Michael never told Jo that he was taking Bibles, but he and Arnaldo took them, having memorized certain addresses where they knew there were Christians. Once they went into a park where Arnaldo played the guitar and sang a few songs to get people interested. Michael had some postcards of Britain and pictures of churches; he spoke to one man at length and slipped him a copy of Mark's Gospel. The man said he would like a Bible and asked if it might be passed to him at a bus stop next morning but he never turned up. Ten years later, when the wall of Communism had fallen down, a Christian working in Albania met a man who asked him if he knew a man called Michael Pollard. 'Yes I do.' 'Then will you tell him', the man continued, 'that ten years ago he gave me a Gospel according to Mark, I read it and I destroyed it because I was fearful that I would be caught and punished. Tell Michael I was converted to Christ through reading that Gospel.'

The great desire of Michael Pollard was that you too, whoever you are, however you have lived, should trust Jesus Christ. Here is a question for each of us here today: *Do you know a man called Michael Pollard?* 'Yes', you reply, 'we knew of Michael Pollard.'

Here is another question: *Do you know a man called Jesus Christ?* Have you ever asked the Christ who died for sin to forgive you and live within you, have you asked the risen living Jesus to be your Lord and Saviour? If not, I would urge you to do so this very day, this very afternoon in this very place.

Suppose the news had not been about Michael Pollard? Suppose that you had died - where would you be now in eternity, in heaven or in hell? None of us deserves heaven; but Christ, who loved us, gave himself for us and is willing to forgive all who come to him and trust him as their Lord and Saviour. I wouldn't be doing justice to Michael's memory or the wishes of the family if I didn't urge you now: 'Ask Jesus to be your Lord, your Saviour, and start to live for him. I plead with you, turn from your sin and trust Christ as Lord and Saviour and one day, you will be with Michael. But more importantly you will be with Michael's Saviour, who will have become your Saviour.'

Endnotes

[1] From *New Zealand Gift of the Sea*, eds Brian Blake and Maurice Shadbolt: Whitcombe and Tombs.
[2] Edmund Burke. Originally, 'These gentle historians, on the contrary, dip their pens in nothing but the milk of human kindness' (*Oxford Dictionary of Quotations* 1979), p.112.
[3] See *Chronicle of the Twentieth Century*: Longman, p.985.
[4] *Daily Sketch*, 22 August 1968.
[5] Richard Wurmbrand, *Tortured for Christ*: Hodder, p.34.
[6] Martha Gellhorn, *The Face of War* (1959).
[7] William Cowper (1731-1800) '*Charity*'.
[8] Joseph Scriven (1819 - 86).
[9] H.W. Longfellow (1807-82) '*A Psalm of Life*'.

If you enjoyed this book you might be interested in the following:

Richard Wurmbrand, *In God's Underground*: Hodder.
Georgi Vins, *Three Generations of Suffering*: Hodder.
Samuel Grandjean, *Genovieva*: Eastern European Aid Association (eeaa@cvn.net)